The Great British Sitcom Quiz Book

Stuart Ball & Lisa Ball

Published by BlackCat Books in association with CreateSpace

Cover image courtesy of Shutterstock

First Published 2013

ISBN: 1481995269
ISBN-13: 978-148199526X

Also available from Stuart Ball and Lisa Ball

Trotter Trivia: The Only Fools and Horses Quiz Book

DEDICATION

In memory of Leslie Ball 1935-2011

Still miss you, Dad.

CONTENTS

ACKNOWLEDGMENTS

We really have to thank all of you lovely people out there who bought a copy of our first book Trotter Trivia, giving us the impetus to go ahead with this new project which you hold in your hands right now.

If this book is a success too, you will probably see more from us in the future. We won't go away that easily, you know!

INTRODUCTION

Comedy shows have been a regular part of the viewing schedules ever since British television was still wearing short trousers. Wait a minute...that was the opening line from the *Trotter Trivia* book, wasn't it? Shame that, because it fits perfectly with the theme of this quiz book too. Oh, what the heck, let's leave it in for this one too!

Of all the various genres within the world of television, comedy remains one of the most popular and easily accessible. Although tastes change over the years, the very best television sitcoms stand the test of the time and remain funny no matter how long ago they were first broadcast. Indeed, many sitcoms seem to grow better with age and perhaps become funnier with repeated viewings.

Audiences also seem to connect more readily with sitcom characters, perhaps seeing a little bit of themselves in a particular character or even a few personality traits of someone they know. How many times, for instance, have you sat down to watch an episode of *The Royle Family* and thought "That's just like my dad, that is" or even "That sounds like something my mum would say"? Anyone who has ever worked in an office is sure to have had the misfortune of coming across a David Brent in their time. If not, that awful company management speak is bound to have reared its very annoying head on more than one occasion!

Despite the continued popularity of television sitcoms, comedy as a whole is undoubtedly the most polarizing of all genres. What one person finds pant-wettingly funny, another may find as hilarious as being stuck in a lift with a House of Lords Select Committee.

This is why, in selecting the 100 sitcoms which feature in this book, we have tried to be as broad as possible. The oldest programme included here was first broadcast in the 1950s while the newest additions are still in production as we speak (or should that be as we write?) No matter if you are a fan of more traditional British comedy such as *Dad's Army*, the biting realism of *The Office* or the over-the-top cartoon violence as often displayed in *Bottom*, *The Great British Sitcom Quiz Book* is sure to have something to suit everyone.

To make it easier to see if your favourite sitcom has been included, all of the sitcoms featured have been arranged into alphabetical order. I know, we're just too kind aren't we?

If your all-time favourite sitcom hasn't been included here, well…we're really sorry! It's been a tough task to narrow it down to just 100. We still hope you enjoy the book though. After all, there's bound to be another favourite sitcom in here for you…

Stuart Ball and Lisa Ball

Official Comedy Nuts and possessors of much useless but nonetheless interesting comedy knowledge.

2POINT4 CHILDREN

BBC1 1991-1999 - 56 episodes

1. What is the surname of the featured family in *2Point4 Children*?

2. The lead characters, played by Belinda Lang and Gary Olsen, share their first names with which famous children's television duo?

3. Which star of *Only Fools and Horses* played the part of Jake Klinger?

4. In which borough of London is the series set?

5. Who created *2Point4 Children* – David Renwick or Andrew Marshall?

6. What are the names of the family's two children?

7. In the 1993 episode *Whoopee We're All Going to Die*, the family are caught in a hurricane while on holiday in which US state?

8. True or False – Liz Smith played two roles in the show, as sisters Bette and Belle?

9. One episode had the same title as a Carry On film. Was it *Carry On Cowboy*, *Carry On Camping* or *Carry On Screaming*?

10. True or False – the very last episode of *2Point4 Children* was a New Year Millennium special?

ABSOLUTELY FABULOUS

BBC1 1992 –2012 - 39 episodes

11. What is the surname of Edina, played by Jennifer Saunders?

12. Which actress played Edina's friend, Patsy Stone?

13. Edina makes her living in which profession?

14. True or False – *Absolutely Fabulous* was based on a sketch which appeared on *French and Saunders*?

15. As well as daughter Saffron, played by Julia Sawalha, Edina has a son. Can you name him?

16. How many times has Edina been married?

17. In the episode *Hospital*, who becomes involved in a sex scandal with a politician?

18. Which room of the house did Patsy once set fire to after falling asleep with a lighted cigarette?

19. True or False – Actress Kate O'Mara made a guest appearance as Edina's elder sister Jackie?

20. At the end of series three, Patsy takes a job as a magazine editor in which American city?

'ALLO 'ALLO

BBC1 1982-1992 - 85 episodes

'Allo 'Allo was renowned for its outlandish, farcical plots and the many catchphrases which it spawned. Can you name the characters associated with the following catchphrases?

21.   You stupid woman!

22.   Leesten very carefully. I shall say zis only once.

23.   Good moaning.

24.   Ooooooh, René!

25.   My dicky ticker!

26.   It is I...

27.   Ze flashing knobs!

28.   What a mistake-a to make-a!

29.   You may kiss me.

30.   'tler!

ARE YOU BEING SERVED?

BBC1 1972-1985 - 69 episodes

31. What is the name of the department store in which *Are You Being Served?* is set?

32. Who was David Croft's writing partner for this series — Jimmy Perry or Jeremy Lloyd?

33. What is the first name of floorwalker Captain Peacock?

34. Which character often refers to her 'pussy'?

35. Which actor played the part of manager Mr Rumbold?

36. In series seven, which character tries to blackmail Captain Peacock by threatening to show an army photograph of him wearing a corporal's uniform?

37. In the episode *The Hand of Fate*, who reveals a talent for palm reading?

38. Which legendary British wrestler appeared in the episode *My Hero* as Mr Franco from the sports department?

39. In the 1977 feature film spin-off of *Are You Being Served?* to which fictional Spanish resort do the department store staff go on holiday?

40. What was the name of the spin-off series of *Are You Being Served?* which first appeared in 1992 and ran for 12 episodes?

THE ARMY GAME

ITV 1957-1961 - 154 episodes

41. What is the name of the barracks in Staffordshire in which the National Service conscripts are based?

42. Which actor, who played the fierce Sgt Major Bullimore, would go on to become the very first Doctor Who?

43. What is the catchphrase of Private 'Popeye' Popplewell, played by future Carry On star Bernard Bresslaw?

44. Which other future member of the Carry On team appeared in two series as Private 'Professor' Hatchett?

45. True or False – Comedian Dick Emery starred in the fifth series as Private 'Chubby' Catchpole?

46. What was the name of the spin-off series from The Army Game featuring the characters of Bill Fraser and Alfie Bass?

47. A feature film based on the series was made in 1958 by which film studios, more famous for their horror output?

48. True or False – The only character to appear in all series of *The Army Game* was 'Popeye' Popplewell?

49. Which future Dad's Army star played the role of Captain Pocket from series three onwards – Arthur Lowe, Frank Williams or Bill Pertwee?

50. The very first Carry On film featured many of the cast from *The Army Game*. What was it called?

AS TIME GOES BY

BBC1 1992-2005 - 66 episodes

51. As played by Judi Dench and Geoffrey Palmer, what are the surnames of the lead characters Jean and Lionel?

52. In the first episode, Jean and Lionel meet up again after not seeing each other for how many years – 28, 38 or 48?

53. What is the name of Jean's only daughter?

54. After his military service, Lionel became a coffee planter in which country?

55. What type of agency does Jean run?

56. What relation is the character Rocky to Lionel?

57. Which star of the Carry On films played Rocky's wife Madge?

58. Alistair, the on-off boyfriend of Jean's daughter, makes his living in which profession?

59. What is the name of Rocky's straight-laced housekeeper, who has a strange obsession with the Shipping Forecast?

60. The classic song *As Time Goes By* was used as the theme tune for the series. Who sang this particular version – Joe Longthorne or Joe Fagin?

BENIDORM

ITV 2007-Present - 35 Episodes

61. What is the name of the all-inclusive hotel where the series is set?

62. Entertainment is provided every evening in which bar?

63. Siobhan Finneran and Steve Pemberton play the mother and father of which family?

64. How is Geoff Maltby, played by Johnny Vegas, better known?

65. What is the name of Geoff's mother?

66. Who wins the arm-wrestling contest in series two by beating barman Mateo in the final?

67. What is the name of the island which Madge's husband Mel tries to buy in series three?

68. Which famous Benidorm entertainment venue do Madge and Mel eventually end up buying?

69. In the first episode of series four, which entertainer is revealed as buying the villa belonging to Madge and Mel?

70. True or False – Benidorm is actually filmed on location in Malaga?

BIRDS OF A FEATHER

BBC1 1989-1998 - 102 episodes

71. At the beginning of the series, Sharon, played by Pauline Quirke, lives in a council flat in which area of London?

72. When their husbands are convicted for armed robbery, Sharon moves in with her sister Tracy in a plush house in which leafy Essex parish?

73. Who plays Sharon and Tracy's neighbour Dorien Green?

74. What is the name of Tracy's eldest son?

75. True or False – Tracy's husband is of Greek Cypriot descent?

76. When Sharon and Tracy decide to set up a cleaning business, what do they call it?

77. In the 1993 Christmas special *It Happened in Hollywood*, Sharon and Tracy are under the illusion their real father is which famous actor?

78. In the same episode, Dorien is mistakenly imprisoned for stalking which star of the sitcom *Cheers*?

79. The theme tune to *Birds of a Feather*, *What'll I Do*, was originally written by which composer – Irving Berlin or Cole Porter?

80. Which two writers created *Birds of a Feather*, in addition to *Goodnight Sweetheart* and *The New Statesman*?

BLACK BOOKS

Channel 4 2000-2004 - 18 episodes

81. Bernard Black's assistant Manny is played by which stand-up comedian?

82. Manny first enters Bernard's shop seeking which book?

83. Which star of *The Office* appeared in the very first episode?

84. In the episode *The Blackout*, Manny has an all-night viewing marathon watching which 70s cop series?

85. What is the name of the rival book shop which opens next door to Black Books at the start of series three?

86. What is Bernard Black's middle name?

87. What is the surname of Bernard and Manny's friend Fran?

88. In the first series, Fran runs a small gift shop. What is it called?

89. Sam Kelly and Annette Crosbie appeared in the episode *Moo-Ma and Moo-Pa* as the parents of which character?

90. Who co-wrote *Black Books* with star Dylan Moran?

THE BLACKADDER

BBC1 1983 - 6 episodes

91. In which century does the action in *The Blackadder* take place?

92. Which legend of British comedy played the role of Richard III?

93. True or False – In the unaired pilot for *The Blackaddder*, the part of Baldrick was played by an actor other than Tony Robinson?

94. What is the name of Edmund's elder brother?

95. In a bid to gain land from the Church, Kind Richard IV appoints Edmund to which exalted position?

96. What is the name of the Spanish Infanta's interpreter – Juan Spakeinglese or Don Speekingleesh?

97. In a memorable episode, the role of the Witchsmeller Pursuivant was played by which classic British actor?

98. In the final episode *The Black Seal*, how many of the 'Most Evil Men of the Kingdom' does Edmund seek out?

99. Who co-wrote this series with Richard Curtis – Ben Elton, Rowan Atkinson or John Lloyd?

100. On the end credits of most episodes, which legendary playwright is credited with providing additional dialogue?

BLACKADDER II

BBC1 1986 - 6 episodes

101. Which noble title does Edmund hold in *Blackadder II*?

102. True or False – It was originally suggested to have the part of Queen Elizabeth I played by Brian Blessed in drag?

103. Which actress finally landed the role of the Queen?

104. What is the real name of the Queen's constant companion Nursie?

105. Which real-life explorer does Edmund try to outdo in the episode *Potato*?

106. In the same episode, which former Doctor Who played the legless sailor Captain Rum?

107. What type of vegetable, formed into a 'rude and amusing shape', does Baldrick serve to the puritanical Lady Whiteadder in the episode *Beer*?

108. Who was once savaged by a turbot?

109. In the final episode *Chains*, what does Baldrick come to the fancy dress party as?

110. True or false – Hugh Laurie played two different roles in *Blackadder II*?

BLACKADDER THE THIRD

BBC1 1987 - 6 episodes

111. What position does Edmund hold in *Blackadder the Third?*

112. Who is the owner of the local coffee shop?

113. In the first episode *Dish and Dishonesty,* who becomes Prime Minister right in the middle of his exams?

114. Who gets promoted to the House of Lords in the same episode?

115. In the episode *Ink and Incapability,* who played Dr Samuel Johnson, author of the first dictionary?

116. Edmund writes his 'rollercoaster of a novel" under which assumed name?

117. True or False – Writer Richard Curtis had a small cameo role in *Sense and Senility* as an anarchist in a theatre?

118. What is the name of Edmund's Scottish cousin?

119. Which famous real-life soldier is played by Stephen Fry in the final episode of the series?

120. According to Edmund, which eccentric King believes himself to be a 'small village in Lincolnshire, commanding spectacular views of the Nene valley'?

BLACKADDER GOES FORTH

BBC1 1989 - 6 episodes

121. *Blackadder Goes Forth* is set during which war?

122. What army rank does Edmund hold?

123. As played by Tim McInnerny, what is Captain Darling's first name?

124. Which silent film comedian does Edmund not find even remotely funny?

125. Who returned to the Blackadder fold with a bang in this series as the irrepressible Lord Flashheart?

126. Who falls in love with Lieutenant George when he dresses as a woman for the troops' concert party?

127. True or False – The role of Nurse Mary in the episode *General Hospital* is played by Miranda Richardson?

128. What is the average life expectancy of a new pilot in the Royal Flying Corps?

129. What is the name of General Melchett's favourite pigeon, who has been with him since he was a child?

130. Which real-life Field Marshall is played by Geoffrey Palmer in the final episode?

BLESS THIS HOUSE

ITV 1971-1976 - 65 episodes

131. What is the surname of the family featured in this series?

132. In which area of London do they live – Putney, Acton or Kensington?

133. Sid James plays head of the household Sid but which of his Carry On co-stars also appeared as neighbour Betty?

134. As played by Diana Coupland, what is the name of Sid's wife?

135. What does Sid do for a living?

136. Who is the eldest of the two children – Mike or Sally?

137. Which pub do Sid and his mate Trevor often frequent?

138. In the film version of *Bless This House*, which of Sid James' Carry On colleagues took over the role of Trevor from Anthony Jackson?

139. Which football team does Sid support?

140. The producer of *Bless This House* went on to present the quiz show *Fifteen to One*. Can you name him?

BOTTOM

BBC2 1991-1995 - 18 episodes

141. What are the surnames of Richie and Eddie, as played by Rik Mayall and Ade Edmondson?

142. In which part of London do Richie and Eddie live?

143. In which pub can you often find Richie and Eddie?

144. What is the name of the pub's landlord?

145. Which future star of the *Pirates of the Caribbean* films appeared in the episode *Smells* as a seedy sex shop owner?

146. In the episode *Culture*, Eddie attempts to teach Richie the rules of which game?

147. Can you name Eddie's two friends, played by Steven O'Donnell and Christopher Ryan?

148. Which comedy actor, more associated with *Red Dwarf*, appeared in the episode *Parade* as a Falklands veteran?

149. In *'S Out*, as a result of losing a bet, Richie and Eddie have to spend a week camping where?

150. After stealing Taffy O'Jones' honeymoon tickets, Richie and Eddie pose as newlyweds at which hotel?

BREAD

BBC1 1986-1991 - 74 episodes

151. In which city of the UK is *Bread* set?

152. What is the name of the family featured in the series?

153. Which female comedy writer created *Bread*?

154. Nellie, the matriarch of the family, was played by which actress?

155. What is the name of Nellie's husband Freddie's mistress?

156. How many children does Nellie have – four, five or six?

157. Which member of the family is a published poet?

158. True or False – Grandad, who lives next door, is Freddie's father?

159. How many actresses played the role of Aveline?

160. What is the name of the family dog?

THE BRITTAS EMPIRE

BBC1 1991-1997 - 53 episodes.

161. Can you name the leisure centre in which this series is set?

162. What is the name of Gordon Brittas' wife?

163. Bizarrely, what does receptionist Carole keep in the drawers behind the reception desk?

164. Which character has a skin condition and an infected hand?

165. In the second episode of series one, which member of the Royal Family is asked to open the leisure centre – Princess Anne or the Duchess of Kent ?

166. In the episode *New Generations,* what kind of farm animal gives birth in the leisure centre's squash court?

167. In the same episode, which member of staff gives birth to twins?

168. When Brittas disguises himself as an elderly customer in *The Stuff of Dreams*, what name does he go by?

169. In the last episode of series five, which main character is killed off, only to be resurrected for two further series?

170. True or False – The very last episode of *The Brittas Empire* reveals all past series to have been a dream had by Gordon?

BRUSH STROKES

BBC1 1986-1991 - 40 episodes

171. The writers of *Brush Strokes* also created *The Good Life* and *Ever Decreasing Circles*. Can you name them?

172. Who performed the show's theme tune, *Because of You*?

173. Which actor played the lead role of painter and decorator Jacko?

174. Gary Waldhorn, who appeared as Lionel Bainbridge in *Brush Strokes*, went on to star in which ecclesiastical sitcom with Dawn French?

175. Who is the rather slow-witted landlord of the local pub?

176. Jacko has a 'will-they won't-they' relationship with the company secretary. Can you name her?

177. What relation is the character Eric to Jacko?

178. What is the name of Lionel's rather spoilt daughter?

179. Actor Mike Walling, who played the role of Eric, appeared in 10 episodes of which long-running soap in 2006?

180. True or False – *Brush Strokes* is set in Newcastle?

BUTTERFLIES

BBC1 1978-1983 - 28 episodes

181. The main character of Ria Parkinson was played by which much-loved actress?

182. What is the profession of Ria's husband Ben?

183. What are the names of Ria's two sons?

184. Which future star of *Only Fools and Horses* played the youngest of those sons?

185. Ria almost embarks on an affair with a rich businessman. Can you name him?

186. What make of car, complete with a Union Jack design on the roof, is featured heavily in the series ?

187. What is the name of Ria's cleaner?

188. Carla Lane, the creator of *Butterflies*, went on to write two sitcoms in the 80s for which star of *The Good Life*?

189. Which of the characters in the series collects butterflies as a hobby?

190. Which legendary female country singer wrote and recorded the original version of the song used as the show's theme, *Love is Like a Butterfly*?

CITIZEN SMITH

BBC1 1977-1980 - 30 episodes

191. Which prolific comedy writer created *Citizen Smith*?

192. As played by Robert Lindsay, Wolfie Smith is the self-proclaimed leader of which revolutionary organization?

193. What is the name of Wolfie's best mate, played by Mike Grady?

194. Wolfie's girlfriend's mum Florence always incorrectly refers to him by which nickname?

195. What is the name of the local pub, run by gangster Harry Fenning ?

196. True or False – The second episode of series three was titled *Only Fools and Horses*?

197. At the end of series three, Wolfie and his revolutionaries use a tank to storm which official building?

198. Actor Peter Vaughn, who played Shirley's dad in the first two series of *Citizen Smith*, previously appeared in *Porridge* as which notorious inmate?

199. True or False – Wolfie is a West Ham supporter?

200. At the end of series four, Wolfie's real first name is revealed. Is it William, Walter or Warren?

DAD'S ARMY

BBC1 1968-1977 - 80 episodes

201. In which fictional seaside town is *Dad's Army* set?

202. What is Captain Mainwaring's daytime profession?

203. Which member of the platoon is a butcher?

204. What is the first name of Private Pike's mum?

205. In which branch of the Armed Forces did Private Frazer serve when he was younger?

206. True or False – *Dad's Army* was originally going to be called *The Fighting Tigers?*

207. What is the name of Captain Mainwaring's wife?

208. Who wrote the lyrics for the show's famous theme tune *Who Do You Think You Are Kidding Mr Hitler?* – Bud Flanagan, Jimmy Perry or Arthur Lowe?

209. When the Home Guard take on the Wardens in a game of cricket in the episode *The Test*, which member of the platoon scores the most runs?

210. In the very last episode *Never Too Old*, which platoon member marries Mrs Fox?

DEAR JOHN

BBC1 1986-1987 - 14 episodes

211. Which actor played the 'John' of the title?

212. True or False – *Dear John* was written by prolific comedy writer Roy Clarke?

213. What is the name of the singles club in which the series is set?

214. What is the name of the leader of the singles club, who always likes to ask "Were there any sexual problems"?

215. In series two, the boring Ralph transforms into DJ Dazzling Darren Dring. Unfortunately he only has one record in his collection – can you name it?

216. Which member of the group sees himself as a ladies man and dresses like John Travolta in *Saturday Night Fever*?

217. John makes his living in which profession – teaching, banking or building ?

218. Which star of *2point4 Children* played the part of group member Kate?

219. Peter Denyer, who played Ralph in *Dear John*, also starred as one of the pupils in which popular school-based sitcom from the late sixties?

220. In the final episode, who rescues Ralph from the clutches of a biker gang?

DESMOND'S

Channel 4 1989-1994 - 71 episodes

221. In which area of London is Desmond's barber shop located?

222. Which actor played the title role of Desmond?

223. What is Desmond's surname?

224. What is the first name of Desmond's wife?

225. Which *Desmond's* character went on to star in their own spin-off series?

226. How many children does Desmond have – two, three or four?

227. Can you name the mature student from Africa who can often be found in the barber shop?

228. Where does Desmond's eldest child Michael work?

229. What is the title of the series' theme tune?

230. Who was the creator and writer of *Desmond's*?

THE DETECTIVES

BBC1 1993-1997 - 31 episodes

231. As played by Robert Powell and Jasper Carrott, what are the first names of Detectives Briggs and Louis?

232. What is comedian Jasper Carrott's real name?

233. Which type of fish, usually sold in a tin, does Louis hate?

234. Which football team does Briggs support?

235. Who is Briggs and Louis' commanding officer?

236. Which comedian and golf fan played suspected arms dealer Johnny McKenna in the episode *Teed Off*?

237. Featuring Leslie Grantham, the episode *Strangers in Paradise* was a parody of which television drama series?

238. In the 1995 Christmas special, the brother of which of our heroes turns up unexpectedly?

239. In *Mine's a Large One*, Briggs and Louis are assigned to which branch of the force as part of a job swap scheme?

240. In the very last episode, Briggs and Louis track down their commanding officer to which country?

DINNERLADIES

BBC1 1998-2000 - 16 episodes

241. Who was the creator and star of *Dinnerladies*?

242. Which actress played the role of Bren's mum Petula?

243. What is the name of the canteen manager?

244. Anne Reid and Thelma Barlow, who played friends Jean and Dolly, both had regular roles in which long-running TV soap?

245. Which character's father is a retired Desert Rat?

246. What is the name of the factory in which the canteen is set?

247. In which city is the factory located?

248. Philippa Moorcroft, played by Celia Imrie, is the manager of which department?

249. Who composed the show's theme tune?

250. What is the name of the TV game show on which Bren hopes to be a contestant?

DROP THE DEAD DONKEY

Channel 4 1990-1998 - 66 episodes

251. What is the name of the television news station in which the series is set?

252. True or False – The original title of the series was *Dead Belgians Don't Count?*

253. What is the name of the media tycoon who buys the station at the beginning of the series, determined to make it more sensationalist?

254. Who is the station's old-fashioned news anchorman?

255. What is the name of his female counterpart?

256. The station's unscrupulous field reporter Damien Day was played by which actor?

257. Which character once said "I'd just like you to stir-fry a few ideas in my strategy wok"?

258. True or False – News editor George Dent was played by Neil Pearson?

259. In the final series, which character was made a god by an Amazonian tribe?

260. Can you name the two writers who created *Drop the Dead Donkey?*

DUTY FREE

ITV 1984-1986 - 22 episodes

261. In which Spanish resort is the action in *Duty Free* set?

262. Which actor played the lead role of David Pearce?

263. As played by Gwen Taylor, what is the name of David's wife?

264. While on holiday, David begins an affair with which character?

265. What is the name of the Spanish waiter who is a regular character in the series?

266. Which former star of *Emmerdale Farm* and *Doctor Who* appeared as himself in the second series episode *El Astro*?

267. In the episode *Close Up*, Judith Chalmers arrives at the hotel to film an episode of which TV series?

268. What is the name of the local bar often frequented by the holidaymakers?

269. In 1986, *Duty Free* was nominated for the BAFTA for Best Comedy Series, eventually losing out to which John Sullivan-penned series?

270. Which writer, who also created *Rising Damp*, co-wrote *Duty Free* with Jean Warr?

EARLY DOORS

BBC2 2003-2004 - 12 episodes

271. What is the name of the pub in which all of the action takes place?

272. Who is the landlord of the pub?

273. Which two inept policeman can often be found in the pub's backroom?

274. In the final episode of the first series, the regulars enjoy a day out at which racecourse, followed by a visit to the Bamboo Club?

275. What is the full name of Melanie's real father?

276. Which future Hollywood actor played the part of Melanie's boyfriend Liam in series one?

277. What is the grand first prize at the pub's quiz night?

278. What is the surname of regulars Eddie and Joan?

279. When Melanie celebrates her 21st birthday in the final episode, which Robbie Williams song does her nan Jean sing on karaoke?

280. Which two cast members created and wrote *Early Doors*?

EVER DECREASING CIRCLES

BBC1 1984-1989 - 27 episodes

281. What is the surname of main character Martin, played by Richard Briers?

282. Which actor played Martin's next-door neighbour and 'rival' Paul?

283. Which two characters always wore 'his and hers' matching outfits?

284. In the episode *Holiday Plans*, Paul offers Martin and Ann the use of his holiday villa in which country?

285. In the episode *Snooker*, who beats Martin in the final of the local snooker tournament?

286. What type of business does Paul initially run?

287. Which tough-guy actor appeared in the first episode of series three – Ray Winstone or Bob Hoskins?

288. What is the name of the company for which Martin works?

289. The theme music used for *Ever Decreasing Circles* was a classical piece composed by who?

290. True or False – In the final feature-length episode, Ann discovers she is pregnant?

EXTRAS

BBC2 2005-2007 - 13 episodes

Ricky Gervais' Extras was famous for attracting many famous guest-stars. For each of the following, answer True or False as to whether they actually appeared in the show or not.

291. JOHNNY DEPP

292. DAVID BOWIE

293. DAME DIANA RIGG

294. DAME HELEN MIRREN

295. RONNIE CORBETT

296. BEN STILLER

297. LIAM NEESON

298. KATE WINSLETT

299. CHARLIE SHEEN

300. SIR IAN MCKELLEN

THE FALL AND RISE OF REGINALD PERRIN

BBC1 1976-1979 - 21 episodes

301. Who played the title character of Reginald Perrin?

302. Which comedy writer created the series?

303. True or False – The character of Reginald Perrin originally appeared in a series of books?

304. For which company does Reggie Perrin work?

305. What is the name of Reggie's boss?

306. Which actress, more famous for her role in *Coronation Street*, played Reggie's secretary Joan?

307. After faking his own death, under what new name does Reggie return?

308. What is the name of the company Reggie establishes which sells totally useless products?

309. Which renowned comedy actor played Reggie's brother-in-law Jimmy?

310. When the character of Reginald Perrin was revived by the BBC for a new series in 2009, who took on the title role?

FATHER TED

Channel Four 1995-1998 - 25 episodes

311. On which island is *Father Ted* set?

312. What are the surnames of Fathers Ted, Dougal and Jack?

313. Which stand-up comedian played the slow-witted Father Dougal?

314. Who is Father Ted's housekeeper?

315. In the very first episode, Father Ted is interviewed for which religious television programme?

316. Which character is thought to have died in the last episode of series one after drinking floor polish?

317. Which comedian and chat-show host played the character of Father Noel Furlong?

318. When Father Jack is sent to an old priest's home in the episode *New Jack City*, what is the name of his replacement?

319. What award is Father Ted presented with, after leading a group of priests out of the lingerie section of a department store in the 1996 Christmas special?

320. After losing a bet, who does Father Ted have to 'kick up the arse'?

FAWLTY TOWERS

BBC1 1975-1979 - 12 episodes

321. In which English seaside resort would you find the Fawlty Towers hotel?

322. Long-suffering waiter Manuel is from which Spanish city?

323. Actor Ballard Berkeley played which permanent resident of the hotel?

324. Which unreliable builder does Basil put his faith in when renovation work is required in the hotel?

325. Who co-wrote *Fawlty Towers* with John Cleese?

326. What is the name of the hotel's chef who featured in series two?

327. In the episode *Communication Problems*, what is the name of the horse that Basil successfully bets on?

328. Which legendary comedy actor played cutlery salesman Mr Hutchinson in the episode *The Hotel Inspectors*?

329. As played by Geoffrey Palmer, hotel guest Dr Price is determined to have what for his breakfast?

330. Which member of the hotel staff is a keen artist?

FILTHY RICH AND CATFLAP

BBC2 1987 - 6 episodes

331. Who played the 'Filthy' of the title?

332. What is Richie's surname?

333. What is the name of the game show on which Richie makes a guest appearance?

334. Which comedian, one half of a famous double act, played the host of the aforementioned game show?

335. What is Eddie Catflap's rather unusual middle name – Boomerang or Didgeridoo?

336. Which all-girl vocal group blackmail Richie after they discover him in their dressing room?

337. Which late comedy actor played Jumbo Whiffy, the Head of Light Entertainment at the BBC?

338. What is the name of the art critic played by Stephen Fry in episode two?

339. Which comedian wrote *Filthy Rich and Catflap*?

340. Which member of the cast provided additional material for the scripts?

FRESH FIELDS

ITV 1984-1986 - 27 episodes.

341. Which two stars played Hester and William, the Fields of the title?

342. What is the name of Hester's busybody friend and next door neighbour?

343. Which actor, more associated with his role in *Fawlty Towers*, played Hester's father Guy?

344. What is the name of the Fields' daughter who has recently left home?

345. What is the profession of William Fields – teacher, accountant or bank manager?

346. In which district of London do the Fields live – Richmond or Barnes?

347. Whose mother lives in a granny flat attached to the Fields' home?

348. True or False – *Fresh Fields* was written by Roy Clarke?

349. Which relaxing leisure activity is William a fan of?

350. True or False – The sequel to *Fresh Fields* was called *Foreign Fields*?

GAVIN AND STACEY

BBC1/BBC3 2007-2010 - 20 episodes

351. In which town in South Wales do Stacey and her family live?

352. What are the names of Gavin's parents?

353. As played by Ruth Jones, what is Nessa's full name?

354. Which *Little Britain* star made a guest appearance in the fourth episode as stag night organizer Jammy?

355. Who played Smithy's mum Cath in series three?

356. Which song do Nessa and Uncle Bryn perform together at Gwen's birthday party?

357. What name do Nessa and Smithy give to their son?

358. Which couple decide to renew their wedding vows in the third series?

359. In the 2008 Christmas special, everybody receives a variation of the same 'gift' from Nessa and Dave. What is it?

360. Which two cast members wrote *Gavin and Stacey*?

GEORGE AND MILDRED

ITV 1976-1979 - 38 episodes

361. *George and Mildred* was a spin-off from which other ITV comedy?

362. What is George and Mildred's surname?

363. Who were George and Mildred's rather well-to-do neighbours?

364. Which fondly remembered comedy actor played George's friend Jerry – Geoffrey Hughes or Roy Kinnear?

365. What is the name of Mildred's Yorkshire Terrier?

366. True or False – George and Mildred's address is 46 Peacock Crescent, Hampton Wick?

367. Famous for her role as Ethel in *EastEnders*, who portrayed Mildred's mother in *George and Mildred*?

368. True or False – Mildred's snobby sister is called Dot?

369. In the 1977 Christmas special, Mildred lands which role in the local pantomime production of *Cinderella*?

370. What type of bird is George's pet, Oscar?

GEORGE AND THE DRAGON

ITV 1966-1968 - 26 episodes

371. Which formidable actress played the Dragon of the title?

372. As played by Sid James, George acts as a chauffeur and handyman to which Colonel?

373. What football team does George support – Arsenal, Chelsea or West Ham?

374. The third member of the Colonel's household staff is Ralph. What job does he do?

375. In the episode *The Unexpected Sport*, George is volunteered to take the Colonel's place in which equestrian team sport?

376. In *The French Lesson*, Gabrielle Dragon wins a trip for two to which city?

377. True or False – The character of George is an inveterate womanizer?

378. In the episode *The TV Set*, George swaps the television channel selector button for the controller off which other household appliance?

379. Which member of the cast suffered a heart attack during the filming of the second series?

380. *George and the Dragon* was written by which writing team – Vince Powell and Harry Driver or Ray Galton and Alan Simpson?

GIMME GIMME GIMME

BBC1/BBC2 1999-2001 - 20 episodes

381. What address do Linda and Tom live at?

382. What is Tom's profession?

383. In the very first episode, Linda and Tom get some new neighbours. Can you name them?

384. Who is Linda and Tom's landlady?

385. As played by former *EastEnders* star Elaine Lordan, what is the name of Linda's celebrity sister?

386. Which prolific comedy actress played singing coach Heidi Honeycomb in the episode *Singing in the Drain*?

387. Which former star of *Peak Practice*, who appeared in a number of episodes of *Gimme Gimme Gimme* as himself, is Tom completely obsessed with?

388. What is the name of the convict who Linda befriends in the episode *Prison Visitor*?

389. Linda has a secret son who turns up on her doorstep after his adoptive parents die. What name did she give him as a baby?

390. When Linda turns the back garden into a campsite, which rather scary former acquaintance decides to stay there?

THE GOOD LIFE

BBC1 1975-1978 - 30 episodes

391. In the opening episode, which milestone birthday is Tom Good celebrating?

392. What is the surname of Margot and Jerry, who live next door to Tom and Barbara?

393. In which suburb of London is this series set?

394. What is the name of Tom and Barbara's goat?

395. What do they call their 'mad' cockerel?

396. Margot stars in which musical at the town hall, a show which gets cancelled after just one night?

397. What is the name of the company for which Tom used to work for and Jerry becomes managing director of in the final episode?

398. When the Good's house becomes infested with fleas in the episode *Whose Fleas are These?*, it turns out that the fleas originated from whose dog?

399. In the 1977 Christmas special, Margot tells everyone that Jerry is suffering from which illness?

400. In the special live episode *When I'm 65*, which veteran comedy actor played the part of the bank manager?

GOODNIGHT SWEETHEART

BBC1 1993-1999 - 58 episodes.

401. What is the surname of Gary, played by Nicholas Lyndhurst?

402. Who is Gary's best friend who runs a printing business?

403. In total, how many actresses played the roles of Gary's wife Yvonne and his wartime mistress Phoebe?

404. What is the name of the pub which Gary frequents during World War II?

405. In the episode *Turned Out Nice Again*, which wartime entertainer wants to record one of Gary's songs?

406. What do Gary and Phoebe call their son, who is actually older than Gary in the present day?

407. Actor David Benson played which real-life flamboyant playwright and actor in a number of later episodes?

408. In the episode *The Leaving of Liverpool*, which future member of The Beatles is described as 'a young boy who can write better songs than Gary'?

409. The creators of *Goodnight Sweetheart*, Laurence Marks and Maurice Gran, also wrote which other wartime comedy drama starring Kenneth Cranham?

410. In the final episode, the time portal closes, leaving Gary stuck permanently in which era – the past or the present?

THE GREEN GREEN GRASS

BBC1 2005-2009 - 32 episodes

411. Boycie moves his family out of Peckham after falling foul of which gangsters?

412. Which Peckham resident warns Boycie of the impending danger in the first episode – Trigger or Denzil?

413. To which county do the Boyce family move?

414. What is the name of the farm which becomes their new home?

415. Who is the eccentric farm manager?

416. What is the name of Boycie and Marlene's Rottweiler?

417. Who forms a rock band called Puddle of Agony?

418. In the final episode *For Richer For Poorer*, Boycie and Marlene celebrate which landmark wedding anniversary?

419. In the same episode, which Tom Jones hit is revealed to be Boycie and Marlene's 'special song'?

420. True or False – *The Green Green Grass* was the first British comedy series to be filmed entirely in HD?

HANCOCK'S HALF HOUR

BBC1 1956-1961 - 63 episodes

421. Which legendary writing duo scripted *Hancock's Half Hour*?

422. At what address does Tony Hancock reside?

423. Who is his rather surly housekeeper?

424. Which regular cast member of the *Hancock's Half Hour* radio series never appeared in a television episode – Bill Kerr, Hattie Jacques or Kenneth Williams?

425. What is the name of the book featured in the classic episode *The Missing Page*?

426. What is the name of the accused in the episode *Twelve Angry Men*?

427. When *Twelve Angry Men* was remade in 1996, which comedian appeared in the Hancock role?

428. Can you name the last television episode to feature Sid James?

429. Who composed the famous *Hancock's Half Hour* theme tune?

430. In which city was Tony Hancock born in real life?

HI-DE-HI

BBC1 1980-1988 - 58 episodes.

431. Which holiday camp is the centrepiece of the action in *Hi-de-Hi?*

432. As played by Paul Shane, who is the resident camp compere?

433. In which decade is *Hi-de-Hi* initially set?

434. In the first episode, who arrives at the camp to take up his position as Entertainments Manager?

435. What is the surname of chalet maid Peggy, who dreams of becoming a Yellowcoat?

436. Who is Peggy's supervisor?

437. What job does grumpy old Mr Partridge fulfil on the entertainment's team?

438. Which member of the Carry On team played the character of Uncle Sammy in later series?

439. True or False – In the final series, Chief Yellowcoat Gladys Pugh and new Entertainments Manager Clive Dempster get married?

440. Who sang *Holiday Rock*, the theme tune to *Hi-de-Hi?*

I DIDN'T KNOW YOU CARED

BBC1 1975-1979 - 27 episodes.

441. In which part of England is this series set – the north or south?

442. Which veteran comedy actress played Annie Brandon?

443. True or False – Annie is Uncle Mort's sister?

444. Which member of the family wears a box around his neck containing the ashes of a dead friend?

445. What is this character's catchphrase from the show?

446. Actor John Comer, who played Annie's husband Les in *I Didn't Know You Cared*, also starred as café owner Sid in which long-running BBC comedy?

447. Which character is laying his wife to rest in the opening episode?

448. Which couple get married at the end of the first series?

449. True or False – *EastEnders* star Anna Wing played semi-regular character Auntie Lil?

450. Which writer scripted *I Didn't Know You Cared*, basing the show on his own series of books?

I'M ALAN PARTRIDGE

BBC2 1997-2002 - 12 episodes

451. At the start of the series Alan Partridge hosts an early-morning show on Radio Norwich. What is it called?

452. Where does he now live, chosen as it is equidistant between London and Norwich?

453. What is the name of the hotel manager?

454. Simon Greenall, who played Michael in *I'm Alan Partridge*, is now the voice of which famous meerkat?

455. In the second series, Alan hosts a military-themed quiz show. What is it called?

456. On which daytime digital channel does this quiz show air?

457. What is the title of Alan's book which takes a look at his return to the big time?

458. Alan's girlfriend Sonja is from which country?

459. In the episode *Never Say Alan Again*, what series of films is Alan planning on watching back-to-back?

460. In the episode *To Kill a Mocking Alan*, what is the name of Alan's 'biggest fan'?

THE INBETWEENERS

E4 2008-2010 - 18 episodes

461. What is the name of the school in which this series is set?

462. Who is the tough head of the sixth form?

463. Which comedian played the character in the previous question?

464. Which character provides the voice-over for each episode?

465. Which member of the group is constantly boasting about his supposed sexual experiences?

466. In the episode *Thorpe Park*, who passes his driving test?

467. What make of car does his dad buy him after passing his test?

468. What is Charlotte Hinchcliffe's nickname?

469. Who inadvertently reveals more of himself than he bargained for when modelling a pair of Speedos in front of the school?

470. In the big-screen version of *The Inbetweeners*, to which Greek holiday resort do the boys travel?

IT AIN'T HALF HOT MUM

BBC1 1974-1981 - 56 episodes

471. *It Ain't Half Hot Mum* is set during which war?

472. In which country is the Royal Artillery Concert Party stationed?

473. What is the name of the fanatical Sergeant-Major?

474. Which popular comedy actor played this character?

475. Which member of the platoon, while short in stature, possesses a beautiful singing voice?

476. Who is the platoon's pianist?

477. True or False – Actor Michael Bates, who played bearer Rangi Ram, was born in India?

478. In the episode *Has Anyone Seen My Cobra?* who finds the snake charmer's missing snake in his quarters?

479. Mrs Waddilove-Evans is the secret lover of which character – Captain Ashwood or Colonel Evans?

480. True or False – *It Ain't Half Hot Mum* was written by Jeremy Lloyd and David Croft?

JUST GOOD FRIENDS

BBC1 1983-1986 - 22 episodes

481. As played by Paul Nicholas and Jan Francis, what are the surnames of Vince and Penny?

482. At the start of the series, how many years has it been since Vince left Penny standing at the altar – three, five or ten?

483. What kind of business does Vince's dad initially run?

484. What are the names of Penny's parents?

485. Who is Vince's rather dim-witted brother?

486. In the final episode of series two, Penny leaves to take up a job in which European city?

487. In the feature-length 1984 Christmas special, it is revealed that Vince and Penny first met at a concert performed by which legendary rock band?

488. What is the name of Vince's wife in series three?

489. True or False – In the final episode, Vince and Penny finally get married?

490. Who sang the theme tune to the series?

KEEPING UP APPEARANCES

BBC1 1990-1995 - 44 episodes

491. Which prolific comedy writer created *Keeping Up Appearances*?

492. Hyacinth likes to tell everyone that her surname is pronounced 'Bouquet' but what is it really?

493. What is the name of Hyacinth's long-suffering husband?

494. What relation is the unseen character Sheridan to Hyacinth?

495. Which character has the catchphrase "Oh, nice…"?

496. Which of the following is not the name of one of Hyacinth's sisters – Rose, Violet or Lily?

497. In the 1993 Christmas special *Sea Fever*, Hyacinth and her husband take a cruise aboard which luxury liner?

498. Which photographer and real-life Lord guest-starred as himself in *Sea Fever*?

499. What are the names of the brother and sister who live next door to Hyacinth?

500. True or False – Patricia Routledge won a Best Light Entertainment Performance BAFTA for her role as Hyacinth?

LAST OF THE SUMMER WINE

BBC1 1973-2010 - 295 episodes

Last of the Summer Wine was renowned for its ensemble cast of veteran
British comedy stars. Can you name the actors who played the
following characters?

501. COMPO SIMMONITE

502. NORMAN CLEGG

503. FOGGY DEWHURST

504. TRULY TRUELOVE

505. ALVIN SMEDLEY

506. NORA BATTY

507. EDIE PEGDEN

508. SMILER HEMMINGWAY

509. MARINA

510. ENTWHISTLE

THE LIVER BIRDS

BBC1 1969-1996 - 87 episodes

511. In which city is this series set?

512. True or False – Nerys Hughes starred as Sandra Hutchinson in every series of *The Liver Birds*?

513. Which actress played Sandra's flatmate Beryl Hennessey?

514. Which legendary comedy actress appeared as Sandra's very snobby mother Mrs Hutchinson?

515. Who created and scripted *The Liver Birds* along with Myra Taylor?

516. When Beryl leaves to get married at the end of series four, who eventually moves in with Sandra as a new flatmate?

517. Appearing in a number of episodes as Sandra's boyfriend Paul, which actor would go on to keep law and order on the island of Jersey in *Bergerac*?

518. What is the name of the street in which the girls' flat is located?

519. In the episode *The Parrot*, which character becomes a vegetarian?

520. As played by Michael Angelis, which character has an obsession with rabbits?

LOVE THY NEIGHBOUR

ITV 1972-1976 - 55 episodes

521. In which area of London is this series set – Tooting, Tottenham or Twickenham?

522. As played by Jack Smethurst and Kate Williams, what are the first names of the Booths?

523. Which comedy actor, now known for his role in *EastEnders*, played the Booth's next door neighbour Bill?

524. What is the name of Bill's wife?

525. True or False – *Love Thy Neighbour* was written by Johnny Speight?

526. Which political party does Bill support?

527. What is the name of the local pub featured in the series?

528. Who is the landlord of the pub – Norris or Nobby?

529. In 1980, a new version of *Love Thy Neighbour* was screened in which country – Australia, New Zealand or Canada?

530. True or False – The big-screen version of *Love Thy Neighbour* was one of the top twenty box-office hits in the UK for the year 1973?

MAN ABOUT THE HOUSE

ITV 1973-1976 - 40 episodes

531. Can you name the actresses who played flatmates Chrissy and Jo?

532. As played by Richard O'Sullivan, what is the surname of Robin who becomes the girls' third flatmate?

533. Robin is a college student training for which profession?

534. Which husband and wife team acted as landlords?

535. Which Hampshire city has Robin recently moved from – Portsmouth or Southampton?

536. What is the name of Robin's brother who appears in series six?

537. Robin's brother begins a romance with which of the girls – Chrissy or Jo?

538. In the episode *Did You Ever Meet Rommel?* which future star of *New Tricks* played Robin's German friend Franz?

539. Which of the main characters gets married in the very last episode?

540. *Three's Company* was the title of a remake of *Man About the House* in which country?

MAX AND PADDY'S ROAD TO NOWHERE

Channel 4 2004 - 6 episodes

541. In the opening episode, who do Max and Paddy purchase a stolen plasma television from?

542. In the same episode, the lads meet Tracey and Louise at a nightclub. What nickname have these girls acquired locally?

543. While in prison, Max's surname is revealed to be the same as which other famous Max?

544. What is Paddy's surname?

545. Which 70s rock star from the Midlands guest-starred in the second episode as dodgy car mechanic Mick Bustin?

546. What are the names of the fictional cops created by Max, based on himself and Paddy?

547. What is the name of Max's son?

548. In prison, Paddy is forced to share a cell with an inmate who is obsessed with which evergreen pop star?

549. What type of farm animal are Max and Paddy desperately trying to sell in episode five?

550. What is the title of the spoof fitness DVD that was a spin-off from *Max and Paddy's Road to Nowhere*?

MAY TO DECEMBER

BBC1 1989-1994 - 39 episodes

551. As played by Anton Rogers, what is the surname of solicitor Alec, who falls in love with a younger woman called Zoe?

552. What is Zoe's profession?

553. When Eve Matheson left the show after the second series, which actress replaced her in the role of Zoe?

554. Which ITV soap opera does this actress currently appear in?

555. What is the name of Alec's senior secretary?

556. The rather dizzy junior secretary Hillary was played by which comedy actress?

557. When Hillary leaves the firm to move to the Isle of Wight at the end of the fifth series, who replaces her at the office?

558. Who secretly writes romance novels under the pseudonym Elvira Storm?

559. When Zoe gives birth to a baby daughter, what do her and proud father Alec name her?

560. True or False – Each episode of *May to December* used the name of a song as its title?

MEN BEHAVING BADLY

BBC1/ITV 1992-1998 - 42 episodes

561. On which channel did *Men Behaving Badly* originally air – BBC1 or ITV?

562. Which comedian played Gary's original flatmate Dermot?

563. As played by Martin Clunes and Neil Morrissey, what are the surnames of Gary and Tony?

564. What is the profession of Gary's girlfriend Dorothy?

565. When Tony first appears in series two, he runs a market stall selling what?

566. What is the name of the pub which Gary and Tony often frequent?

567. Who is the original landlord of the pub?

568. In the episode *Lovers*, what is the grand prize on offer at the pub quiz night?

569. Binki, Sod and Plop are all names of what?

570. In a special Comic Relief episode from 1997, which Australian pop princess turns up on the doorstep of the flat?

MIND YOUR LANGUAGE

ITV 1977-1986 - 42 episodes

571. What is the name of the English teacher played by Barry Evans?

572. Actor Ricardo Montez played a student from which country?

573. Dino Shafeek, who played Pakistani student Ali Nadim, also had a regular role in which military-themed sitcom of the seventies?

574. Who is the headmistress of the adult education college?

575. What is the name of the French student played by Françoise Pascal?

576. True or False – Indian student Ranjeet Singh works as a bus driver?

577. Which familiar comedy character actor played college caretaker Sid – Arthur English, Tommy Godfrey or Alfie Bass?

578. Which character has the catchphrases "Holy Ravioli" and "Okey-kokey"?

579. With only a very basic knowledge of English, from which country does Zoltan Szabo originate?

580. True or False – When *Mind Your Language* was revived for a final series in 1986, none of the original students appeared?

MIRANDA

BBC1/BBC2 2009 – present - 18 episodes

581. Which popular comedy actress plays the title role?

582. *Miranda* started life as a comedy series on which BBC radio station?

583. What type of shop does Miranda run?

584. What is the name of Miranda's childhood friend who acts as the manager of the shop?

585. Miranda's mother Penny is played by which veteran television actress?

586. Which character often interrupts conversations with the phrase "Bear with…"?

587. In series three, Miranda has a new love interest called Mike. What is Mike's job?

588. In the very first episode *Date*, Miranda tries to impress long-term crush Gary by telling him she has two children. What does she profess their names to be?

589. Which former Doctor Who played school teacher Mr Clayton in the episode *Teacher*?

590. Which Tom starred as Miranda's dad in the special episode *The Perfect Christmas* – Tom Courtenay or Tom Conti?

MRS BROWN'S BOYS

BBC1 2011 – present - 21 episodes

591. Who is the star, creator and writer of *Mrs Brown's Boys*?

592. Who is Agnes Brown's best friend and neighbour?

593. What is the name of the family dog?

594. Can you name the eldest of Mrs Brown's children?

595. In an attempt to impress Maria's rather snobbish mother, what does Agnes have installed in her house?

596. Who acts as best man at Dermot and Maria's wedding?

597. What is Maria's maiden name?

598. What is the name of the fake animal charity used in a raffle ticket scam in the episode *Mammy's Merchandise*?

599. Which local pub do the Brown family frequent?

600. Which couple get married in the final episode of series three?

MY FAMILY

BBC1 2000-2011 - 120 episodes

601. What is the name of the featured family in this series?

602. What is the profession of Ben, played by Robert Lindsay?

603. Which actress played Ben's wife Susan?

604. How many children do Ben and Susan have?

605. In which area of London do Ben and Susan live?

606. Actor Kris Marshall received his big break playing which character?

607. Who has a baby called Kenzo in series four?

608. Which star of *Only Fools and Horses* made a guest appearance in the 2007 Christmas special *Ho Ho No*?

609. The 2009 Christmas special was set how many years into the future – 20. 30 or 40?

610. In series ten, which character reveals their homosexuality?

MY HERO

BBC1 2000-2006 - 51 episodes.

611. True or False – *My Hero* is set in Northolt in London?

612. Which day of the week also happens to be the surname of superhero Thermoman's mild-mannered alter ego George?

613. How do Thermoman and nurse Janet first meet?

614. What type of shop is George the proprietor of?

615. As played by Hugh Dennis, what is the name of the narcissistic doctor who also happens to be Janet's boss?

616. Who is the ferocious receptionist at the medical centre?

617. What planet is Thermoman from?

618. In the episode *A Little Learning*, what type of 'magic' snack food turns George into an intellectual genius?

619. In which New York borough does George's Uncle Arnie live?

620. When Ardal O'Hanlon left the show after five series, which comedy actor replaced him in the role of Thermoman?

NEVER THE TWAIN

ITV 1981-1991 – 67 episodes

621. Simon Peel and Oliver Smallbridge are neighbours and rival dealers in which trade?

622. Can you name the two actors who played these characters?

623. What is the name of Oliver Smallbridge's rather slow-witted assistant?

624. After Simon's son and Oliver's daughter get married, to which country do they emigrate?

625. What is the name of Simon's butler, played by Teddy Turner?

626. Clumsy, accident-prone cleaner Mrs Charles works for who – Simon or Oliver?

627. The first two series saw Simon and Oliver fighting for the affections of widow Veronica Barton. Which former Bond girl played Veronica?

628. What is the name of Simon and Oliver's baby grandson?

629. In the show's title sequence, Simon Peel is portrayed as a noble bust while Oliver Smallbridge is what object?

630. Which prolific comedy scriptwriter created *Never the Twain* – Vince Powell, Johnnie Mortimer or Eric Chappell?

THE NEW STATESMAN

ITV 1987-1994 - 29 episodes

631. Alan B'stard is an MP for which political party?

632. What is Alan B'stard's middle name?

633. This middle name is shared with which real life political figure – Norman Tebbit, Margaret Thatcher or Tony Benn?

634. Actor John Nettleton, who played Sir Stephen Baxter in *The New Statesman*, also had a regular role in which other political sitcom?

635. Which character was played by Michael Troughton?

636. What is the name of Alan's wife?

637. Played by Peter Sallis, local pub landlord Sidney Bliss was the last man in Britain to be employed in which job role?

638. In the episode *Keeping Mum*, Alan's mother ruins a dinner party he has organised for which Royal couple?

639. In the episode *A Bigger Splash*, Alan purchases a luxury yacht which was formerly owned by which controversial media mogul?

640. True or False – *The New Statesman* was created and written by Laurence Marks and Maurice Gran?

NO PLACE LIKE HOME

BBC1 1983-1987 - 43 episodes

641. What is the surname of the family featured in *No Place Like Home?*

642. Head of the family Arthur was played by which actor?

643. As played by Patricia Garwood, what is the name of Arthur's wife?

644. How many children do Arthur and his wife have – three, four or five?

645. Which future star of *Men Behaving Badly* appeared here as youngest son Nigel?

646. In addition to his children returning home, Arthur's peace is often disturbed by his next door neighbour? Can you name her?

647. What is the name of this character's husband, who also happens to be Arthur's best friend?

648. Which prolific television music composer provided the theme tune for this series?

649. Creator of *No Place Like Home* Jon Watkins also scripted a number of episodes of which other domestic sitcom – *Terry and June* or *Bless This House?*

650. True or False – *No Place Like Home* was originally entitled *Home to Roost?*

NOT GOING OUT

BBC1 2006 – present - 42 episodes

651. As played by comedian Lee Mack, the character of Lee is originally from which Lancashire town?

652. What is the surname of Lee's best mate Tim?

653. In series one, Lee lodges with Tim's ex-girlfriend Kate. What country was Kate born in?

654. What relationship is Lucy to Tim?

655. Which veteran comic plays Lee's no-good father Frank?

656. What type of establishment does Lucy's boyfriend Guy run in series two?

657. In which series does Tim's rather slow-witted girlfriend Daisy first appear – one, two or three?

658. What is the name of the girl who turns up on Lee's doorstep believing him to be her father?

659. In the episode *Band*, what is the name of the rock band which Tim becomes a member of?

660. True or False – In the non-broadcast pilot episode of *Not Going Out*, the part of Kate was played by Catherine Tate?

THE OFFICE

BBC1 / BBC2 2001-2003 - 14 episodes

661. What is the name of the paper merchants featured in *The Office*?

662. Who co-wrote this series alongside Ricky Gervais?

663. Who is the company receptionist?

664. What is Tim's surname?

665. David Brent has always considered himself an entertainer. What is the name of the band for which he used to be singer/songwriter?

666. At the start of series two, the Slough office is merged with the branch from which town?

667. What does David Brent name his dog?

668. In the episode *The Quiz*, who acts as question master during the annual quiz night?

669. During the same episode, new recruit Ricky reveals he was once a contestant on which television quiz show?

670. David is told he is being made redundant on which special day?

ON THE BUSES

ITV 1969-1973 - 74 episodes

671. What is the surname of bus driver Stan, played by Reg Varney?

672. Stan's conductor and best mate Jack was played by which actor?

673. True or False – Arthur, played by Michael Robbins, is Stan's brother?

674. Which comedy actor played Stan's nemesis Inspector Blake?

675. What is the name of the bus company featured in the series?

676. What is the number of the bus that Stan regularly drives?

677. Which two cast members teamed up to write a number of episodes during later series?

678. When the series ended in 1973, which main character went on to star in his own spin-off sitcom called *Don't Drink the Water*?

679. Which film company, more associated with horror films, produced three *On the Buses* spin-off films during the 1970s?

680. True or False – The first *On the Buses* film was the top-box office earner in UK cinemas for 1971, even beating James Bond?

ONE FOOT IN THE GRAVE

BBC1 1990-2000 - 42 episodes

681. Grumpy pensioner Victor Meldrew was played by which actor?

682. What is the name of Victor's long-suffering wife?

683. Which comedy writer created *One Foot in the Grave*?

684. The show's theme tune was written and performed by which member of the Monty Python team?

685. At what age does Victor take early retirement?

686. Which couple live next door to Victor from series two onwards?

687. In the episode *The Return of the Speckled Band*, who accidentally drinks carpet shampoo believing it to be an indigestion remedy?

688. In the same episode, what type of creature accidentally finds its way into the Meldrew's holiday luggage?

689. The 1990 Christmas special saw the Meldrew's house overrun by what kind of garden ornament?

690. Which member of The Goodies appeared in the 1997 Christmas special *Endgame*?

ONLY FOOLS AND HORSES

BBC1 1981-2003 - 64 episodes

691. In which area of London do the Trotter family live?

692. The tower block in which their flat is located is named after which famous world figure?

693. What is Rodney's middle name?

694. Can you name the episode in which Uncle Albert first makes an appearance?

695. Which couple live in the affluent King's Avenue?

696. Who was Trigger referring to when he said "He made one great film and then you never saw him again."?

697. Who is the eldest brother – Grandad or Uncle Albert?

698. In the 1991 Christmas special, Del is mistaken for a mafia boss while holidaying in which American city?

699. What is the name of the television game show hosted by Jonathan Ross on which Del is a contestant?

700. In the final episode *Sleepless in Peckham*, who is revealed to be the real father of Rodney?

ONLY WHEN I LAUGH

ITV 1979-1982 - 29 episodes

701. What is the first name of long-term hospital patient Figgis, played by James Bolam – Roy, Fred or Brian?

702. Which prolific comedy actor played hypochondriac Archie Glover?

703. What is the name of the Indian ward orderly?

704. Christopher Strauli played the third of the featured patients. Can you name the character?

705. In the episode *Is There a Doctor in the House?* which of the patients gets mistaken for a doctor?

706. What is the surname of the doctor played by *One Foot in the Grave* star Richard Wilson?

707. Which former Doctor Who guest-starred in the episode *When There's a Will* – Patrick Troughton or Jon Pertwee?

708. Who is told he needs a blood transfusion in the episode *Blood Brothers?*

709. True or False – In the final episode, all three patients are discharged?

710. Who was the creator and writer of *Only When I Laugh?*

OPEN ALL HOURS

BBC1/BBC2 1976-1985 - 26 episodes

711. What is the seldom mentioned first name of miserly shopkeeper Arkwright?

712. What relation is Granville to Arkwright?

713. What is the profession of Gladys Emmanuel, played by Lynda Baron?

714. Regular customer Mrs Featherstone is known by what rather fearsome nickname?

715. Which regular customer is forever undecided on which products to purchase?

716. Mrs Blewett was played by which star of *Last of the Summer Wine*?

717. When Arkwright advertises for a live-in housekeeper in the episode *The Housekeeper Caper*, who applies for the position, much to his horror?

718. Although the identity of Granville's father is unknown, Arkwright believes he may have been from which country?

719. *Open All Hours* started life as a one-off episode in which Ronnie Barker comedy showcase series?

720. In which South Yorkshire town were the exterior scenes of Arkwright's shop filmed?

PHOENIX NIGHTS

Channel Four 2001-2002 - 12 episodes

721. In which northern town is the Phoenix Club situated?

722. What is the name of the rival club run by Brian Potter's nemesis Den Perry?

723. Who is the regular compere at the Phoenix Club?

724. What is the name of the club's backing band?

725. In the very first episode, which real-life television personality is on hand to help re-open the Phoenix Club?

726. Which star of *Auf Wiedersehen Pet* appeared in the same episode as the lead singer of racist folk band Half a Shilling?

727. What is the name of the Right Said Fred tribute band which Brian Potter hires for the Talent Trek evening?

728. Who becomes licensee of the Phoenix Club when it re-opens after being partially destroyed by fire?

729. Alongside Peter Kay and Dave Spikey, which other member of the *Phoenix Nights* cast wrote the scripts for the series?

730. In the final episode, the club holds a Stars in Their Eyes evening. Who causes quite a stir by appearing on stage dressed as Britney Spears?

PLEASE SIR!

ITV 1968-1972 - 55 episodes

731. In which school is the action in *Please Sir!* set?

732. Which actor played inexperienced teacher Bernard Hedges?

733. Which unruly class was Hedges put in charge of?

734. As played by comedy veteran Deryck Guyler, what job did the belligerent Norman Potter have at the school?

735. Peter Denyer, who played slow-witted pupil Dennis Dunstable, later appeared as Ralph in which John Sullivan-penned bittersweet comedy?

736. What is the name of the school headmaster?

737. The formidable deputy head was played by which comedy actress?

738. True or False – A big-screen version of *Please Sir!* was released in 1971?

739. Can you name the spin-off series from *Please Sir!* which followed the lives of some of the pupils after they left school?

740. *Please Sir!* was created by which comedy writing partnership?

PORRIDGE

BBC1 1974-1977 - 20 episodes

741. In which fictitious prison is *Porridge* set ?

742. How many years behind bars is Norman Stanley Fletcher sentenced to?

743. When Fletch first arrives at the prison, who are the other two inmates who arrive with him?

744. What is the name of the judge who passes sentence on Fletch and then ends up sharing a cell with him in series three?

745. An almost unrecognisable David Jason appears in three episodes of Porridge. What is the name of his character?

746. Which comedy actor played kindly prison officer Mr Barrowclough?

747. Who is the governor of the prison?

748. In the episode *Just Desserts*, what type of tinned fruit goes missing from Fletcher's cell?

749. In the episode *A Test of Character*, in which subject is Godber hoping to gain a qualification?

750. Can you name each of Fletch's three children?

RAB C NESBITT

BBC2 1990-2011 - 64 episodes

751. What is Rab's real first name?

752. In which district of Glasgow do Rab and his family live?

753. How many sons do Rab and his wife Mary have?

754. Which of these sons died in a ramming accident?

755. What is the name of Rab's best friend, played by Tony Roper?

756. In which local pub do the regular characters often gather during the first eight series?

757. In later series, Mary and Ella start a cleaning business. What is it called?

758. What is the name of Rab and Mary's granddaughter?

759. In the 2011 episode *Broke,* which distinguished actor played government minister Chingford Steel – Charles Dance, Richard E Grant or Kenneth Branagh?

760. Which former Doctor Who star played Rab's long-lost brother Gash Snr. in the episode *Father?*

THE RAG TRADE

BBC1/ITV 1961-1978 - 58 episodes

761. What is the name of the clothing firm featured in *The Rag Trade*?

762. Which prolific comedy actor played the firm's boss?

763. True or False - Works foreman Reg was played by *On The Buses* star Reg Varney?

764. What is the catchphrase of shop steward Paddy, played by Miriam Karlin?

765. Which diminutive actress, who also appeared in four *Carry On* films during the 1960s, played the character of Lily?

766. Another *Carry On* star who appeared in *The Rag Trade* was Barbara Windsor. Can you name her character?

767. When *The Rag Trade* was revived for ITV in 1977, who performed the theme tune – Bonnie Tyler or Lynsey De Paul?

768. True or False – *The Rag Trade* was created by Dick Clement and Ian La Frenais?

769. Who replaced Reg as works foreman in the later ITV series?

770. Which future *EastEnders* star appeared in later episodes as Lyn?

RED DWARF

BBC2/Dave 1988-2012 - 61 episodes

Red Dwarf has had a number of guest stars appear over the years. For each
of the following, answer True or False as to whether they have ever
featured in a Red Dwarf episode.

771. JENNY AGUTTER

772. ROBERT POWELL

773. ANITA DOBSON

774. GERALDINE McEWAN

775. TIMOTHY SPALL

776. DAVID TENNANT

777. ROBERT GLENISTER

778. DON WARRINGTON

779. JANE HORROCKS

780. SIMON DAY

RISING DAMP

ITV 1974-1978 - 28 episodes

781. What is the first name of miserly landlord Rigsby?

782. As played by Richard Beckinsale, what is Alan studying at university?

783. What is the name of Rigsby's cat?

784. Which tenant of the house claims to be the son of an African tribal king?

785. How many wives does this character claim to have – five, ten or twelve?

786. True or False – The character of Rigsby was originally called Rooksby?

787. In the episode *Stand Up and Be Counted*, which political party is Rigsby canvassing for?

788. Miss Jones is the object of Rigsby's affection but can you remember her first name?

789. Which comedy actress played Miss Jones?

790. What is the title of the original play on which *Rising Damp* was based?

ROBIN'S NEST

ITV 1977-1981 - 48 episodes

791. In which comedy series did the character of Robin Tripp first appear?

792. In which area of London is the Robin's Nest bistro situated?

793. What is the name of the one-armed Irishman employed to do the washing-up?

794. Which actress played Robin's girlfriend/wife Vicky?

795. True or False – Tony Britton played Robin's father James in the series?

796. Where is Vicky working at the beginning of the series?

797. Who goes into partnership with Robin to open the bistro?

798. Which former Bond girl appeared occasionally as Vicky's mother in earlier episodes?

799. Robin's Nest was created by Brian Cooke and which other comedy writer?

800. Which member of the cast wrote the theme tune to the series?

THE ROYLE FAMILY

BBC1/BBC2 1998-2012 - 25 episodes

801. How many children do Jim and Barbara Royle have?

802. What is the name of the unseen local pub which the Royles often frequent?

803. What does Denise's husband Dave do for a living?

804. What is the full name, including middle names, of Denise and Dave's first child?

805. Which former politician and TV talk show host does Jim refer to as "orange-gob"?

806. In the opening episode, Jim is horrified to discover that someone in the house has been making phone calls to which Scottish city?

807. When next door neighbour Joe injures his hand grating cheese, his wife Mary states they will return to using which product, citing it to be a "much safer cheese"?

808. In a classic episode, Jim and best mate Twiggy dance to which song while stripping wallpaper?

809. In the 2009 Christmas special *The Golden Egg Cup*, Jim, Barbara, Denise and Dave take a caravan holiday in which Welsh seaside resort?

810. Used as the theme tune to *The Royle Family*, the song *Half the World Away* is performed by which band?

SHELLEY

ITV 1979-1992 - 71 episodes

811. What is the first name of 'freelance layabout' Shelley, played by Hywell Bennett?

812. Which prolific comedy actress played Shelley's landlady Mrs Hawkins?

813. Which former star of *Randall and Hopkirk Deceased* appeared in the first series as job centre employee Alan Forsyth?

814. What is the name of Shelley's girlfriend, played by Belinda Sinclair?

815. True or False – By the end of the third series, Shelley and his girlfriend have married and had a baby?

816. After a gap of four years, Shelley returned to the screen in 1988. To which country had his former girlfriend now moved?

817. The new series saw Shelley living in shared accommodation with which upwardly mobile couple?

818. In the final two series, Shelley moves in with a pensioner. Can you name him?

819. When *Shelley* was revived for a BBC Radio 2 series in 1997, who took over the title role – Paul Merton, Stephen Tompkinson or John Thomson?

820. True or False – *Shelley* was created by writer Peter Vincent?

THE SMOKING ROOM

BBC Three 2004-2005 - 17 episodes

821. The character of Robin, who seems to be a permanent fixture in the smoking room, was played by which comedy actor?

822. Robin is infatuated with which worker from the post-room?

823. What is the name of the foul-mouthed security guard?

824. The episode *Chocolate Box* takes place on which day of the year?

825. In the 2004 Christmas special, Lilian provides the finale for the old folks' Christmas show by performing as which singer?

826. On the same show, who takes on the role of Joseph for the Nativity scene?

827. In the very first episode, the occupants of the smoking room are desperately trying to remember the theme tune to which TV series?

828. Which character celebrates their birthday in the final episode of series one?

829. Which real-life entertainment duo are jokingly listed on the sign-up sheet for the company paintball excursion?

830. Selina Griffiths, who played the role of personal assistant Janet in *The Smoking Room*, is the daughter of which actress?

SOME MOTHERS DO 'AVE 'EM

BBC1 1973-1978 - 22 episodes

831. Which actor played the lead role of accident-prone Frank Spencer?

832. What is the name of Frank's long-suffering wife?

833. Can you remember the name of Frank's baby daughter?

834. What type of hat was Frank often seen wearing?

835. True or False – The role of Frank Spencer was originally offered to Norman Wisdom?

836. The 1975 Christmas special revolves around Frank learning to do what – drive, fly or ride a bike?

837. In the final series, Frank's long-lost grandfather returns and offers to take Frank away to a new life in which country?

838. Actress Michelle Dotrice, who played Frank's long-suffering wife, was married to which actor in real life?

839. Who was the creator and writer of this series?

840. True or False – Music maestro Ronnie Hazlehurst composed the theme tune to *Some Mother's Do 'Ave 'Em* by spelling out the letters in the title in Morse code?

SORRY!

BBC1 1981-1988 - 42 episodes

841. Which diminutive comedian took the lead role of Timothy Lumsden in this series?

842. What is Timothy's occupation?

843. What is the first name of Timothy's overbearing and domineering mother?

844. What is the often-heard catchphrase of Timothy's father Sydney?

845. Timothy's sister managed to escape the clutches of their mother and get married. Can you remember the names of both her and her husband?

846. In the episode *Buttons*, Tim lands the part of the rear end of a horse in which pantomime production?

847. What is the name of Tim's best friend, played by Roy Holder?

848. What are the surnames of writing due Ian and Peter, who created *Sorry*?

849. William Moore, who played henpecked Sydney Lumsden, was in real life married for many years to which veteran comedy actress – Beryl Reid, Dora Bryan or Mollie Sugden?

850. True or False – The part of Timothy Lumsden was first offered to Ronnie Barker who turned it down?

SPACED

Channel 4 1999-2001 - 14 episodes

851. *Spaced* was created and written by Simon Pegg in conjunction with which actress?

852. What is the surname of Simon Pegg's character Tim?

853. Which comedy actor played Tim's best friend Mike?

854. What is the address of the building in which Tim and Daisy rent a flat?

855. Who is the landlady at this address?

856. In what type of establishment does Tim work?

857. Who once commandeered a tank and tried to invade the city of Paris?

858. In the episode *Art*, what is the unusual name of the performance artist played by David Walliams?

859. In the episode *Change*, Tim is fired from his job for spouting negative comments about which film?

860. What is the name of Daisy's pet dog?

STEPTOE AND SON

BBC1 1962-1974 - 57 episodes

861. What is the street address of the residence of Albert and Harold Steptoe?

862. In which area of London is this address?

863. What is the name of the Steptoe's faithful horse?

864. Who has the middle name Kitchener – Harold or Albert?

865. Which school did Harold attend as a child?

866. In the episode *The Economist*, Harold buys 4000 sets of what?

867. Which British comedy great played the part of escaped prisoner Johnny in *The Desperate Hours*?

868. What is the name of Albert's eldest brother, who is revealed to have died in the episode *Oh, What a Beautiful Mourning*?

869. What is the title of the second *Steptoe and Son* film, released in 1973?

870. Which legendary writing partnership created and wrote the scripts for *Steptoe and Son*?

SYKES

BBC1 1972-1979 - 68 episodes

871. As played by Eric Sykes and Hattie Jacques, how were the characters of Eric and Hattie related in the series?

872. At what address do Eric and Hattie live?

873. What name do Eric and Hattie give to the bird inside their cuckoo clock?

874. As played by Deryck Guyler, what is the nickname of PC Turnbull?

875. Which other female member of the Carry On team occasionally appeared alongside Hattie Jacques in *Sykes* as Madge Kettlewell?

876. Which legend of British comedy appeared in the 1972 episode *Stranger* as escaped prisoner and old acquaintance Tommy Grando?

877. The episode *Football* saw which real-life TV sports presenter guest-star as himself – Des Lynam, Jimmy Hill or Frank Bough?

878. What is the name of Eric and Hattie's snooty neighbour, played by Richard Wattis?

879. Which comedian, famous for his huge moustache, appeared in the episode *Job*?

880. True or False – The scripts for *Sykes* were all written by Spike Milligan?

TERRY AND JUNE

BBC1 1979-1987 - 65 episodes

881. As played by Terry Scott and June Whitfield, what is the surname of the title couple?

882. This series was mostly a reworking of which other sitcom starring the same couple, which ended just a year before *Terry and June* began?

883. Terry works for a company which makes what kind of safety equipment?

884. True or False - The owner of the company was played by actor Reginald Marsh, who also played Jerry's boss in *The Good Life*?

885. What is the name of Terry and June's rarely seen daughter?

886. The opening episode sees Terry and June move into a new house in which area of London?

887. In the 1985 Christmas special *Pantomania*, Terry and June land the role of a cow in which pantomime?

888. Which actor, well-known for playing Charlie Hungerford in *Bergerac*, appeared in the first two series of *Terry and June* as Terry's co-worker Malcolm?

889. True or False – A feature-length *Terry and June – The Movie* was planned but never made it to production?

890. The majority of episodes were scripted by which writer – John Kane, Barry Cryer or Dave Freeman?

THE THIN BLUE LINE

BBC1 1995-1996 - 14 episodes

891. *The Thin Blue Line* is set in the police station of which town?

892. What is the first name of Inspector Fowler, played by Rowan Atkinson?

893. Which actor played the excitable PC Goody?

894. Goody has a long-standing crush on which fellow officer?

895. Inspector Fowler enjoys reading stories featuring which famous fictional sleuth?

896. In the episode *Rag Week*, Fowler foils a bank robbery by disguising himself as what?

897. In the episode *Kids Today*, Rowan Atkinson is joined by which fellow *Blackadder* cast member, playing the role of Brigadier Blaster Sump?

898. The 1995 Christmas special *Yuletide Spirit* sees Inspector Fowler desperate to land which part in the amateur dramatic society's production of *Peter Pan*?

899. Having been turned down by the Masons, Detective Inspector Grim tries his luck at joining which other secret society?

900. Who replaced DC Kray as Grim's number two in the second series?

TILL DEATH US DO PART

BBC1 1965-1975 - 54 episodes

901. Which actor portrayed the opinionated Alf Garnett, becoming synonymous with the role in the process?

902. Alf is a passionate supporter of which football team?

903. Often called a 'silly old moo' by Alf, what is the first name of the long-suffering Mrs Garnett, played by Dandy Nicholls?

904. Actor Anthony Booth, who played Alf's son-in-law Mike, later became the father-in-law of which British Prime Minister?

905. When Dandy Nicholls became too ill to appear in the series, her character went to look after her sick sister in which country?

906. Which comedian appeared in a 1974 episode as the half-Irish, half-Indian Kevin O'Grady, a character who also appeared in the series *Curry and Chips*?

907. In the episode *The Royal Wedding*, Alf tries to organise a street party to celebrate the wedding of which member of the Royal Family?

908. Which political party is Alf a staunch supporter of?

909. Running from 1985 to 1992, what was the title of the follow-up series to *Till Death Us Do Part*?

910. What was the name of Alf's home help in this new series?

TO THE MANOR BORN

BBC1 1979-2007 – 22 episodes

911. What is the name of the stately home featured in this series?

912. Which comedy actress played the lead role of Audrey fforbes-Hamilton?

913. As played by Peter Bowles, new keeper of the manor Richard DeVere is owner of which supermarket chain?

914. In which country was Richard DeVere born?

915. What is the name of Audrey's loyal and long-serving butler?

916. What breed of dog is Audrey's pet Bertie?

917. What affectionate nickname is given to Richard's mother, as her surname is so difficult to pronounce?

918. What is the name of the estate gardener, who temporarily becomes Audrey's butler?

919. The final series sees Richard trying to buy a new refrigeration plant for his company in which South American country?

920. When the series returned for a one-off Christmas special in 2007, how many years of marriage were Audrey and Richard celebrating?

TWO PINTS OF LAGER AND A PACKET OF CRISPS

BBC2/BBC Three 2001-2011 - 80 episodes

921. This series is set in which town in Cheshire?

922. Cast members Will Mellor and Natalie Casey had previously appeared together in which soap opera?

923. Can you name the couple played by Ralf Little and Sheridan Smith?

924. Donna's mother Flo was played by which *Coronation Street* star?

925. As played by Will Mellor, what does Gaz do for a living?

926. What is the name of the local pub where the main characters can often be found?

927. Who is the real father of Janet's baby Corinthian?

928. Which character is killed off at the beginning of series seven, perishing after going shark-jumping in Hawaii?

929. What is the name of Gaz's half-brother?

930. First appearing in series eight, what is the surname of Donna's new boyfriend Wesley?

UP POMPEII!

BBC1/ITV 1969-1991 - 16 episodes

931. Which legendary comedian was the star of *Up Pompeii!*, playing the part of Roman slave Lurcio?

932. What is the name of the Senator who is Lurcio's master?

933. Can you remember the name of the Senator's voluptuous wife?

934. In the episode *The Ides of March*, Lurcio turns out to be an exact lookalike of which Roman Emperor?

935. Which comedian, satirist and regular panel-show guest played Roman playwright Plautus in the first series?

936. True or False – The Senator's daughter was called Erotica?

937. The 1971 big-screen version of *Up Pompeii!* saw which actor take on the role of Lurcio's master?

938. Who played Roman soldier Bilius in the same film?

939. Inspired by *Up Pompeii!*, what is the title of the 1973 series set in ancient Iraq, which accounted the adventures of servant Ali Oopla?

940. *Up Pompeii!*, with its double-entendres and saucy one-liners, was scripted by which writer, famous for writing the majority of the Carry On film series?

THE VICAR OF DIBLEY

BBC1 1994-2007 - 20 episodes

941. What is the name of the local church in the village of Dibley?

942. Who does Geraldine replace as Vicar of Dibley, after he dies aged 102?

943. Who is the head of the Parish Council, who initially opposes Geraldine's appointment as Vicar?

944. Which veteran comedy actress played the queen of bad cooking Letitia Cropley?

945. Who comes out of the closet while hosting a show on Radio Dibley?

946. In the classic 1996 Christmas special *The Christmas Lunch Incident*, Geraldine eats four Christmas dinners because she hates to say no. Who does she have lunch with first?

947. In the same episode, Alice buys Geraldine a biography of which girl group as a Christmas present?

948. In the episode *Celebrity Vicar*, Geraldine is invited onto the Pause for Thought slot on whose radio show?

949. Which pop star saves the day in the episode *Community Spirit* by opening the annual Dibley Autumn Fair?

950. In the final episode *The Vicar in White*, Geraldine gets married to a village newcomer. Can you name the bridegroom?

WAITING FOR GOD

BBC1 1990-1994 - 47 episodes

951. What is the name of the retirement home featured in the series?

952. Can you remember the surnames of Diana and Tom, played by Stephanie Cole and Graham Crowden?

953. Who is the penny-pinching, ineffectual manager of the retirement home?

954. True or False - Diana is a retired photojournalist who specialised in covering war zones?

955. True or False - Tom is a retired teacher?

956. The retirement home is situated near to which seaside town — Eastbourne, Bournemouth or Skegness?

957. Which resident is forever trying to seduce the ladies, even though he is well into his seventies?

958. The incredibly dull Geoffrey is son to who — Tom or Diana?

959. The theme music for *Waiting for God* is a piece taken from the *Trout Quintet* by which Austrian composer?

960. In 1992, Stephanie Cole took the Best TV Comedy Actress honour for her role as Diana at which annual awards?

WHATEVER HAPPENED TO THE LIKELY LADS?

BBC1 1973-1974 - 27 episodes

961. In the opening episode, who is returning home after a stint in the army?

962. How many years has he served – three, five or seven?

963. In what sort of establishment does Bob's fiancée/wife Thelma work?

964. In the classic episode *No Hiding Place*, Bob and Terry desperately try to avoid hearing the result of the England football match so that they can watch the highlights on TV. Which country are England due to play?

965. What is the name of Terry's sister?

966. Susan Chambers is sister to who – Bob or Thelma?

967. Which member of the *Last of the Summer Wine* cast played Thelma's father George?

968. Which actress, famous for her portrayal of Miss Marple, played Thelma's mother in the first series?

969. Bob and Thelma decide to spend their honeymoon skiing in which country?

970. Which member of the pop group Manfred Mann co-wrote the series theme tune *Whatever Happened to You*?

YES MINISTER

BBC1 1980-1984 - 22 episodes

971. *Yes Minister* was reputedly the favourite show of which real-life Prime Minister?

972. In the opening episode, Jim Hacker, played by Paul Eddington, is appointed as the minister for which Government department?

973. Which actor memorably portrayed Jim Hacker's scheming Permanent Secretary, Sir Humphrey Appleby?

974. As played by Derek Fowlds, what is the name of Hacker's Private Secretary?

975. Which future star of *Coronation Street* played Sir Frederick, otherwise known as Jumbo, in series one?

976. Annie is the wife of who – Jim Hacker or Sir Humphrey?

977. Which member of The Goodies appeared in the episode *The Death List* as security adviser Commander Forrest?

978. The episode *The Right to Know* sees Jim Hacker's daughter Lucy concerned about the fate of which wild animal – fox, badger or rabbit?

979. In the 1984 Christmas special *Party Games*, Hacker becomes the front-runner in the race to be the new Prime Minister after delivering a passionate speech on which humble food item?

980. True or False – *Yes Minister* was the first programme to win the BAFTA for Best Comedy Series three years in a row?

YES PRIME MINISTER

BBC1 1986-1988 - 16 episodes

981. Upon taking his position as Prime Minister, who does Jim Hacker appoint as his political adviser?

982. What is the name of the Permanent Secretary to the Treasury and Sir Humphrey's main rival in becoming Head of the Civil Service?

983. Sir Humphrey often seeks the advice of the former Cabinet Secretary, now retired. Can you remember his name?

984. What position does Bill Pritchard hold in relation to the Prime Minister?

985. In the episode *A Conflict of Interest*, Jim Hacker is manoeuvred into appointing who as the new Governor of the Bank of England?

986. Which prolific comedy actress appeared in the episode *Power to the People* as militant council leader Agnes Moorhouse – Joan Sims, June Whitfield or Gwen Taylor?

987. In the episode *A Tangled Web*, who unwittingly reveals more than he would wish when a microphone is left on after a radio interview has finished?

988. Which real-life political broadcaster and journalist played himself in the same episode?

989. Who co-wrote *Yes Prime Minister* and its predecessor *Yes Minister* along with Antony Jay?

990. In the updated version of *Yes Prime Minister*, first broadcast on GOLD in 2013, who portrayed Jim Hacker?

THE YOUNG ONES

BBC2 1982-1984 - 12 episodes

991. What is the name of the college that Rik, Vyvyan, Neil and Mike attend?

992. Which comedian portrayed the various members of the Balowski family?

993. What type of animal is Vyvyan's pet, SPG?

994. What do the letters SPG stand for?

995. What is the name of the pub that the lads visit in the episode *Boring*?

996. Rik is a huge fan of which evergreen pop star?

997. *The Young Ones* was famous for featuring a musical act in each episode. Who were the only band to appear on two separate occasions?

998. Coloured bright yellow with red flames painted on the side, what make of car does Vyvyan own?

999. Revealed in the episode *Sick*, what is Neil's surname?

1000. Can you name the four stars who played the members of the Footlights College, Oxbridge team on University Challenge in the episode *Bambi*?

ANSWERS

2Point4 Children

1. Porter
2. Bill and Ben
3. Roger Lloyd Pack
4. Chiswick
5. Andrew Marshall
6. Jenny and David
7. Florida
8. True
9. Carry On Screaming
10. True

Absolutely Fabulous

11. Monsoon
12. Joanna Lumley
13. Public Relations
14. True
15. Serge
16. Twice
17. Patsy
18. Kitchen
19. False – Jackie is Patsy's elder sister
20. New York

'Allo 'Allo

21. René Artois
22. Michelle of the Resistance
23. Officer Crabtree
24. Yvette
25. Monsieur Alfonse
26. LeClerc
27. Madame Fanny
28. Captain Bertorelli
29. Herr Flick
30. Captain Hans Geering

Are You Being Served?

31. Grace Brothers
32. Jeremy Lloyd
33. Stephen
34. Miss Slocombe
35. Nicholas Smoth
36. Mr Goldberg
37. Mr Humphries
38. Jackie Pallo
39. Costa Plonka
40. Grace and Favour

The Army Game

41. Nether Hopping
42. William Hartnell
43. "I only arsked!"
44. Charles Hawtrey
45. True
46. Bootsie and Snudge
47. Hammer
48. False – No characters managed to last the entire run
49. Frank Williams
50. Carry On Sergeant

As Time Goes By

51. Pargetter and Hardcastle
52. 38
53. Judith
54. Kenya
55. Secretarial
56. Father
57. Joan Sims
58. Publishing
59. Mrs Bale
60. Joe Fagin

Benidorm

61. Solana
62. Neptune's
63. The Garveys
64. The Oracle
65. Noreen
66. Martin
67. Peacock Island
68. Benidorm Palace
69. Cilla Black
70. False – it is filmed in Benidorm

Birds of a Feather

71. Edmonton
72. Chigwell
73. Lesley Joseph
74. Garth
75. False – it is Sharon's husband who is of that descent
76. Maids of Ongar
77. George Hamilton
78. George Wendt
79. Irving Berlin
80. Laurence Marks and Maurice Gran

Black Books

81. Bill Bailey
82. The Little Book of Calm
83. Martin Freeman
84. The Sweeney
85. Goliath Books
86. Ludwig
87. Katzenjammer
88. Nifty Gifty
89. Manny
90. Graham Linehan

The Blackadder

91. 15th
92. Peter Cook
93. True – In the pilot, Baldrick was played by Philip Fox
94. Prince Harry
95. Archbishop of Canterbury
96. Don Speekingleesh
97. Frank Finlay
98. Six
99. Rowan Atkinson
100. William Shakespeare

Blackadder II

101. Lord
122. True
103. Miranda Richardson
104. Bernard
105. Sir Walter Raleigh
106. Tom Baker
107. Turnip
108. Percy
109. A pencil case
110. True – Simon Partridge in *Beer* and Prince Ludwig in *Chains*

Blackadder the Third

111. Butler to the Prince Regent
112. Mrs Miggins
113. Pitt the Younger
114. Baldrick
115. Robbie Coltrane
116. Gertrude Perkins
117. False – It was Ben Elton
118. MacAdder
119. Duke of Wellington
120. George III

Blackadder Goes Forth

121. World War I
122. Captain
123. Kevin
124. Charlie Chaplin
125. Rik Mayall
126. General Melchett
127. True
128. Twenty minutes
129. Speckled Jim
130. Field Marshal Douglas Haig

Bless This House

131. Abbott
132. Putney
133. Patsy Rowlands
134. Jean
135. Stationery salesman
136. Mike
137. The Hare and Hounds
138. Peter Butterworth
139. Chelsea
140. William G. Stewart

Bottom

141. Richard and Hitler
142. Hammersmith
143. The Lamb and Flag
144. Dick Head
145. Kevin R. McNally
146. Chess
147. Spudgun and Dave Hedgehog
148. Robert Llewellyn
149. Wimbledon Common
150. Marveloso Splendido Hotelo in Wolverhampton

Bread

151. Liverpool
152. Boswell
153. Carla Lane
154. Jean Boht
155. Lilo Lill
156. Five
157. Adrian
158. False – He is Nellie's father
159. Two
160. Mongy

The Brittas Empire

161. Whitbury New Town
162. Helen
163. Her children
164. Colin
165. Duchess of Kent
166. Cow
167. Carole
168. Derek Didcott
169. Gordon Brittas
170. True

Brush Strokes

171. John Esmonde and Bob Larbey
172. Dexys Midnight Runners
173. Karl Howman
174. The Vicar of Dibley
175. Elmo
176. Sandra
177. Brother-in-law
178. Lesley
179. Coronation Street
180. False – It is set in London

Butterflies

181. Wendy Craig
182. Dentist
183. Russell and Adam
184. Nicholas Lyndhurst
185. Leonard
186. Mini
187. Ruby
188. Felicity Kendal
189. Ben
190. Dolly Parton

Citizen Smith

191. John Sullivan
192. Tooting Popular Front
193. Ken
194. Foxy
195. The Vigilante
196. True
197. Houses of Parliament
198. Harry Grout
199. False – He supports Fulham
200. Walter

Dad's Army

201. Walmington-on-Sea
202. Bank manager
203. Lance Corporal Jones
204. Mavis
205. Navy
206. True
207. Elizabeth
208. Jimmy Perry
209. Sergeant Wilson
210. Lance Corporal Jones

Dear John

211. Ralph Bates
212. False – It was written by John Sullivan
213. 1-2-1 Club
214. Louise
215. Green Door by Shakin' Stevens
216. Kirk
217. Teaching
218. Belinda Lang
219. Please Sir
220. Kirk

Desmond's

221. Peckham
222. Norman Beaton
223. Ambrose
224. Shirley
225. Porkpie
226. Three
227. Matthew
228. In a bank
229. Don't Scratch My Soca
230. Trix Worrell

The Detectives

231. Dave and Bob
232. Robert Davis
233. Pilchards
234. Manchester United
235. Superintendent Frank Cottam
236. Jimmy Tarbuck
237. The Paradise Club
238. Louis
239. River Police
240. Canada

Dinner Ladies

241. Victoria Wood
242. Julie Walters
243. Tony
244. Coronation Street
245. Stan
246. HWD Components
247. Manchester
248. Human Resources
249. Victoria Wood
250. Totally Trivial

Drop the Dead Donkey

251. GlobeLink News
252. True
253. Sir Royston Merchant
254. Henry Davenport
255. Sally Smedley
256. Stephen Tompkinson
257. Gus Hedges
258. False – He was played by Jeff Rawle
259. Damien Day
260. Andy Hamilton and Guy Jenkin

Duty Free

261. Marbella
262. Keith Barron
263. Amy
264. Linda
265. Carlos
266. Frazer Hines
267. Wish You Were Here
268. Pedro's
269. Just Good Friends
270. Eric Chappell

Early Doors

271. The Grapes
272. Ken
273. Phil and Nigel
274. York
275. Keith Braithwaite
276. James McAvoy
277. A box of chocolates
278. Bell
279. Angels
280. Craig Cash and Phil Mealey

Ever Decreasing Circles

281. Bryce
282. Peter Egan
283. Howard and Hilda
284. Spain
285. Howard
286. Hairdressing salon
287. Ray Winstone
288. Mole Valley Valves
289. Shostakovich
290. True

Extras

291. False
292. True
293. True
294. False
295. True
296. True
297. False
298. True
299. False
300. True

The Fall and Rise of Reginald Perrin

301. Leonard Rossiter
302. David Nobbs
303. True
304. Sunshine Desserts
305. CJ
306. Sue Nicholls
307. Martin Welbourne
308. Grot
309. Geoffrey Palmer
310. Martin Clunes

Father Ted

311. Craggy Island
312. Crilly, McGuire and Hackett
313. Ardal O'Hanlon
314. Mrs Doyle
315. Faith of Our Fathers
316. Father Jack
317. Graham Norton
318. Father Stack
319. Golden Cleric
320. Bishop Brennan

Fawlty Towers

321. Torquay
322. Barcelona
323. Major Gowen
324. Mr O'Reilly
325. Connie Booth
326. Terry
327. Dragonfly
328. Bernard Cribbins
329. Sausages
330. Polly

Filthy Rich and Catflap

331. Nigel Planer
332. Rich
333. Ooer! Sounds a Bit Rude!
334. Gareth Hale
335. Didgeridoo
336. The Nolans
337. Mel Smith
338. Alphonse P'Farty
339. Ben Elton
340. Rik Mayall

Fresh Fields

341. Julia McKenzie and Anton Rodgers
342. Sonia
343. Ballard Berkeley
344. Emma
345. Accountant
346. Barnes
347. Hester's
348. False – It was written by John Chapman
349. Fishing
350. False – It was called *French Fields*

Gavin and Stacey

351. Barry
352. Pam and Mick
353. Vanessa Shanessa Jenkins
354. Matt Lucas
355. Pam Ferris
356. Islands in the Stream
357. Neil
358. Pete and Dawn
359. A single Celebrations chocolate
360. Ruth Jones and James Corden

George and Mildred

361. Man About the House
362. Roper
363. The Fourmiles
364. Roy Kinnear
365. Truffles
366. True
367. Gretchen Franklin
368. False – Her name is Ethel
369. An Ugly Sister
370. Budgie

George and the Dragon

371. Peggy Mount
372. Colonel Maynard
373. Arsenal
374. Gardener
375. Polo
376. Paris
377. True
378. Cooker
379. Sid James
380. Vince Powell and Harry Driver

Gimme Gimme Gimme

381. 69 Paradise Passage, Kentish Town
382. Actor
383. Jez and Suze
384. Beryl
385. Sugar Walls
386. Su Pollard
387. Simon Shepard
388. Freddie Windrush
389. Zippy
390. Shirley Twitch

The Good Life

391. 40th
392. Leadbetter
393. Surbiton
394. Geraldine
395. Lenin
396. The Sound of Music
397. JJM
398. Mrs Dooms-Paterson
399. Chickenpox
400. George Cole

Goodnight Sweetheart

401. Sparrow
402. Ron
403. Four
404. The Royal Oak
405. George Formby
406. Michael
407. Noel Coward
408. John Lennon
409. Shine On Harvey Moon
410. Past

The Green Green Grass

411. The Driscoll Brothers
412. Denzil
413. Shropshire
414. Winterdown
415. Elgin Sparrowhawk
416. Earl
417. Tyler
418. 40th
419. What's New Pussycat?
420. True

Hancock's Half Hour

421. Ray Galton and Alan Simpson
422. 23 Railway Cuttings, East Cheam
423. Mrs Cravatte
424. Bill Kerr
425. Lady Don't Fall Backwards
426. John Harrison Peabody
427. Paul Merton
428. The Poison Pen Letters
429. Wally Stott
430. Birmingham

Hi-de-Hi

431. Maplins
432. Ted Bovis
433. 1950s
434. Jeffrey Fairbrother
435. Ollerenshaw
436. Miss Cathcart
437. Children's Entertainer
438. Kenneth Connor
439. True
440. Paul Shane

I Didn't Know You Cared

441. The North
442. Liz Smith
443. True
444. Uncle Stavely
445. "I heard that! Pardon?"
446. Last of the Summer Wine
447. Uncle Mort
448. Carter and Pat
449. False – It was Gretchen Franklin
450. Peter Tinniswood

I'm Alan Partridge

451. Up with the Partridge
452. Linton Travel Tavern
453. Susan
454. Aleksandr Orlov
455. Skirmish
456. UK Conquest
457. Bouncing Back
458. Ukraine
459. The James Bond films
460. Jed Maxwell

The Inbetweeners

461. Rudge Park Comprehensive
462. Mr Gilbert
463. Greg Davies
464. Will
465. Jay
466. Simon
467. Fiat Cinquecento Hawaii
468. Big Jugs
469. Simon
470. Malia

It Ain't Half Hot Mum

471. World War II
472. India
473. Sergeant-Major Williams
474. Windsor Davies
475. Lofty Sugden
476. Gunner Graham
477. True
478. Sergeant-Major Williams
479. Colonel Evans
480. False – It was written by Jimmy Perry and David Croft

Just Good Friends

481. Pinner and Warrender
482. Five
483. Scrap metal merchants
484. Daphne and Norman
485. Clifford
486. Paris
487. The Rolling Stones
488. Gina
489. True
490. Paul Nicholas

Keeping Up Appearances

491. Roy Clarke
492. Bucket
493. Richard
494. Son
495. Onslow
496. Lily
497. QE2
498. Lord Lichfield
499. Emmet and Elizabeth
500. False – She was nominated twice but did not win.

Last of the Summer Wine

501. Bill Owen
502. Peter Sallis
503. Brian Wilde
504. Frank Thornton
505. Brian Murphy
506. Kathy Staff
507. Dame Thora Hird
508. Stephen Lewis
509. Jean Fergusson
510. Burt Kwouk

The Liver Birds

511. Liverpool
512. False – She was not in series one
513. Polly James
514. Molly Sugden
515. Carla Lane
516. Carol
517. John Nettles
518. Huskisson Street
519. Sandra
520. Lucien

Love Thy Neighbour

521. Twickenham
522. Eddie and Joan
523. Rudolph Walker
524. Barbie
525. False – It was created by Vince Powell and Harry Driver
526. Conservative
527. The Lion and Lamb
528. Nobby
529. Australia
530. True

Man About the House

531. Paula Wilcox and Sally Thomsett
532. Tripp
533. Chef/Catering
534. George and Mildred
535. Southampton
536. Norman
537. Chrissy
538. Dennis Waterman
539. Chrissy
540. USA

Max and Paddy's Road to Nowhere

541. Gypsy Joe
542. The Belgrano Sisters
543. Max Bygraves
544. O'Shea
545. Noddy Holder
546. Magnet and Steel
547. Daniel
548. Cliff Richard
549. Pig
550. Max and Paddy's The Power of Two

May to December

551. Callender
552. PE teacher
553. Lesley Dunlop
554. Emmerdale
555. Miss Flood
556. Rebecca Lacey
557. Rosie
558. Miss Flood
559. Fleur
560. True

Men Behaving Badly

561. ITV
562. Harry Enfield
563. Strang and Smart
564. Nurse
565. Records
566. The Crown
567. Les
568. All the pork scratchings you can eat in five minutes
569. Beers of the World
570. Kylie Minogue

Mind Your Language

571. Mr Brown
572. Spain
573. It Ain't Half Hot Mum
574. Miss Courtney
575. Danielle Favre
576. False – He is a London Underground worker
577. Tommy Godfrey
578. Giovanni
579. Hungary
580. False – There were four original students in the final series

Miranda

581. Miranda Hart
582. Radio Two
583. Joke shop
584. Stevie
585. Patricia Hodge
586. Tilly
587. TV news reporter
588. Orlando and Bloom
589. Peter Davison
590. Tom Conti

Mrs Brown's Boys

591. Brendan O'Carroll
592. Winnie McGoogan
593. Spartacus
594. Mark
595. A downstairs toilet
596. Buster Brady
597. Nicholson
598. The Dublin Home for Bewildered Greyhounds and Whippets
599. Foleys
600. Rory and Dino

My Family

601. Harper
602. Dentist
603. Zoe Wanamaker
604. Three
605. Chiswick
606. Nick
607. Janey
608. John Challis
609. 30
610. Michael

My Hero

611. True
612. Sunday
613. He rescues her when she falls into the Grand Canyon
614. Health food shop
615. Dr Piers Crispin
616. Mrs Raven
617. Ultron
618. Pork scratchings
619. Brooklyn
620. James Dreyfus

Never the Twain

621. Antiques
622. Donald Sinden and Windsor Davies
623. Ringo
624. Canada
625. Banks
626. Oliver
627. Honor Blackman
628. Martin
629. Toby Jug
630. Johnnie Mortimer

The New Statesman

631. Conservative
632. Beresford
633. Norman Tebbit
634. Yes Minister
635. Piers Fletcher-Dervish
636. Sarah
637. Hangman
638. Duke and Duchess of York
639. Robert Maxwell
640. True

No Place Like Home

641. Crabtree
642. William Gaunt
643. Beryl
644. Four
645. Martin Clunes
646. Vera
647. Trevor
648. Ronnie Hazelhurst
649. Terry and June
650. False

Not Going Out

651. Chorley
652. Adams
653. USA
654. Sister
655. Bobby Ball
656. Lap Dancing Club
657. Two
658. Debbie
659. The Auditors
660. True

The Office

661. Wernham Hogg
662. Stephen Merchant
663. Dawn
664. Canterbury
665. Foregone Conclusion
666. Swindon
667. Nelson
668. Gareth
669. Blockbusters
670. Comic Relief Day

On the Buses

671. Butler
672. Bob Grant
673. False – He is his brother-in-law
674. Stephen Lewis
675. Luxton and District
676. 11
677. Bob Grant and Stephen Lewis
678. Blakey
679. Hammer Films
680. True

One Foot in the Grave

681. Richard Wilson
682. Margaret
683. David Renwick
684. Eric Idle
685. 60
686. Patrick and Pippa
687. Mrs Warboys
688. Snake
689. Garden Gnomes
690. Tim Brooke-Taylor

Only Fools and Horses

691. Peckham
692. Nelson Mandela
693. Charlton
694. Strained Relations
695. Boycie and Marlene
696. Gandhi
697. Grandad
698. Miami
699. Goldrush
700. Freddie "The Frog" Robdal

Only When I Laugh

701. Roy
702. Peter Bowles
703. Gupte
704. Norman Binns
705. Figgis
706. Thorpe
707. Patrick Troughton
708. Archie
709. True
710. Eric Chappell

Open All Hours

711. Albert
712. Uncle
713. Nurse
714. The Black Widow
715. Mavis
716. Kathy Staff
717. Mrs Featherstone
718. Hungary
719. Seven of One
720. Doncaster

Phoenix Nights

721. Bolton
722. The Banana Grove
723. Jerry St. Clair
724. Les Alanos
725. Roy Walker
726. Tim Healy
727. Right Said Frank
728. Jerry
729. Neil Fitzmaurice
730. Kenny Senior

Please Sir

731. Fenn Street Secondary School
732. John Alderton
733. 5C
734. Caretaker
735. Dear John
736. Mr Cromwell
737. Joan Sanderson
738. True
739. The Fenn Street Gang
740. John Esmonde and Bob Larbey

Porridge

741. Slade
742. Five
743. Godber and Heslop
744. Stephen Rawley
745. Blanco Webb
746. Brian Wilde
747. Mr Venables
748. Pineapple chunks
749. History
750. Ingrid, Marion and Raymond

Rab C Nesbitt

751. Robert
752. Govan
753. Two
754. Burney
755. Jamesie
756. The Two Ways Inn
757. The Squeaky Clean House Mice
758. Peaches
759. Richard E Grant
760. Sylvester McCoy

The Rag Trade

761. Fenner Fashions
762. Peter Jones
763. True
764. "Everybody out!"
765. Esma Cannon
766. Judy
767. Lynsey De Paul
768. False – It was created by Ronald Wolfe and Ronald Chesney
769. Tony
770. Gillian Taylforth

Red Dwarf

771. True
772. False
773. True
774. True
775. True
776. False
777. False
778. True
779. True
780. False

Rising Damp

781. Rupert
782. Medicine
783. Vienna
784. Philip
785. Ten
786. True
787. Conservative
788. Ruth
789. Frances de la Tour
790. The Banana Box

Robin's Nest

791. Man About the House
792. Fulham
793. Albert Riddle
794. Tessa Wyatt
795. False – He played Vicky's father James
796. Airport
797. James
798. Honor Blackman
799. Johnnie Mortimer
800. Richard O'Sullivan

The Royle Family

801. Two
802. The Feathers
803. Removals man
804. David Keanu Ronan Best
805. Robert Kilroy-Silk
806. Aberdeen
807. Dairy Lea
808. Mambo No. 5 by Lou Bega
809. Prestatyn
810. Oasis

Shelley

811. James
812. Josephine Tewson
813. Kenneth Cope
814. Fran
815. True
816. Canada
817. Graham and Carol
818. Ted
819. Stephen Tompkinson
820. False – It was created by Peter Tilbury

The Smoking Room

821. Robert Webb
822. Ben
823. Len
824. Valentine's Day
825. Cher
826. Barry
827. Little House on the Prairie
828. Lilian
829. Ant and Dec
830. Annette Crosbie

Some Mothers Do 'Ave 'Em

831. Michael Crawford
832. Betty
833. Jessica
834. Beret
835. True
836. Drive
837. Australia
838. Edward Woodward
839. Raymond Allen
840. True

Sorry

841. Ronnie Corbett
842. Librarian
843. Phyllis
844. "Language, Timothy!"
845. Muriel and Kevin
846. Cinderella
847. Frank
848. Davidson and Vincent
849. Mollie Sugden
850. False

Spaced

851. Jessica Stevenson
852. Bisley
853. Nick Frost
854. 23 Meteor Street, Tufnell Park
855. Marsha Klein
856. Comic book store
857. Mike
858. Vulva
859. Stars Wars Episode I: The Phantom Menace
860. Colin

Steptoe and Son

861. Oil Drum Lane
862. Sheperd's Bush
863. Hercules
864. Harold
865. Scrubs Lane Elementary School
866. False teeth
867. Leonard Rossiter
868. George
869. Steptoe and Son Ride Again
870. Ray Galton and Alan Simpson

Sykes

871. Brother and sister
872. 28 Sebastopol Terrace, East Acton
873. Peter
874. Corky
875. Joan Sims
876. Peter Sellers
877. Frank Bough
878. Charles Fulbright-Brown
879. Jimmy Edwards
880. False – The scripts were all written by Eric Sykes

Terry and June

881. Medford
882. Happy Ever After
883. Fire extinguishers
884. True
885. Wendy
886. Purley
887. Jack and the Beanstalk
888. Terence Alexander
889. True
890. John Kane

The Thin Blue Line

891. Gasforth
892. Raymond
893. James Dreyfus
894. Maggie Habib
895. Sherlock Holmes
896. A pizza delivery man
897. Stephen Fry
898. Captain Hook
899. The Todgers
900. DC Boyle

Till Death Us Do Part

901. Warren Mitchell
902. West Ham United
903. Else
904. Tony Blair
905. Australia
906. Spike Milligan
907. Princess Anne
908. Conservatives
909. In Sickness and In Health
910. Winston

To The Manor Born

911. Grantleigh Manor
912. Penelope Keith
913. Cavendish Foods
914. Czechoslovakia
915. Brabinger
916. Beagle
917. Mrs Poo
918. Ned
919. Argentina
920. 25 years

Two Pints of Lager and a Packet of Crisps

921. Runcorn
922. Hollyoaks
923. Jonny and Janet
924. Beverley Callard
925. Mechanic
926. The Archer
927. Gaz
928. Jonny
929. Munch
930. Presley

Up Pompeii!

931. Frankie Howerd
932. Ludicrus Sextus
933. Ammonia
934. Julius Caesar
935. Willie Rushton
936. True
937. Michael Hordern
938. Lance Percival
939. Whoops Baghdad
940. Talbot Rothwell

The Vicar of Dibley

941. St Barnabas'
942. Rev. Pottle
943. David Horton
944. Liz Smith
945. Frank Pickle
946. Jim and Frank
947. The Spice Girls
948. Terry Wogan
949. Kylie Minogue
950. Harry Kennedy

Waiting for God

951. Bayview Retirement Home
952. Trent and Ballard
953. Harvey Baines
954. True
955. False – He is a retired accountant
956. Bournemouth
957. Basil Makepeace
958. Tom
959. Schubert
960. British Comedy Awards

Whatever Happened to The Likely Lads?

961. Terry
962. Five
963. Library
964. Bulgaria
965. Audrey
966. Thelma
967. Bill Owen
968. Joan Hickson
969. Norway
970. Mike Hugg

Yes Minister

971. Margaret Thatcher
972. Administrative Affairs
973. Nigel Hawthorne
974. Bernard Woolley
975. John Savident
976. Jim Hacker
977. Graeme Garden
978. Badger
979. Sausage
980. True

Yes Prime Minister

981. Dorothy Wainwright
982. Sir Frank Gordon
983. Sir Arnold Robinson
984. Press Officer
985. Sir Desmond Glazebrook
986. Gwen Taylor
987. Sir Humphrey
988. Ludovic Kennedy
989. Jonathan Lynn
990. David Haig

The Young Ones

991. Scumbag College
992. Alexei Sayle
993. Hamster
994. Special Patrol Group
995. The Kebab and Calculator
996. Cliff Richard
997. Madness
998. Ford Anglia
999. Pye
1000. Ben Elton, Stephen Fry, Hugh Laurie and Emma Thompson

www.ingramcontent.com/pod-product-compliance
Lightning Source LLC
Chambersburg PA
CBHW071354310526
45790CB00017B/383